Steal Away!

Essays on why blacks

should reconsider

their allegiance to

the Democratic Party

Edited

and with

an Introduction

by

Richard Showstack

Steal Away!

Steal Away!

"Steal Away" was a black spiritual that communicated that the person singing it was planning to escape from slavery. It was composed by Wallace Willis, a slave of a Choctaw freedman in the old Indian Territory, sometime before 1862.

* * * * * * * * * * * * * * * * * * * *

The Words to "Steal Away"

Chorus: steal away, steal away!

Steal away to Jesus?
Steal away, steal away home!
I ain't got long to stay here!

My Lord calls me!
He calls me by the thunder!
The trumpet sound it in my soul!
I ain't got long to stay here!

Chorus

My Lord calls me!
He calls me by the lighting!
The trumpet sound it in my soul!
I ain't got long to stay here!

Steal Away!

Acknowledgements

I would like to express my
deep appreciation to everyone who contributed to this
endeavor. None of them was
paid for their contributions.

Richard Showstack

Table of Contents

Introduction by Richard Showstack   1

Essays

Why Blacks Must Stop Voting
    Democrat, by Lloyd Marcus   72

Steal Away to Freedom —
    Escape The Democratic Party
    Plantation, Sure: But to where?
    by Armstrong Williams   84

The Destruction of the Black Family
    Unit, the Fake Crimes Bill and
    the Emptiness of the Obama Era,
    by Kevin Martin   93

The Democratic Party Should Not Be
    the Only Party for Black People,
    by Jerome Danner   105

Justifiably Proud: The Standing of
    Blacks in the Republican Party,
    by W.B. Allen   112

Why am I a Conservative Republican?

by Mike Hill 124

Wake Up, Walk Away, and

Don't Look Back!

by Emery W. McClendon 133

The Apotheosis of Black Conser-

vatism and the Escape from

the Democrat Party Plantation,

by Stone Allen Washington 144

Why Not a Black Political Party?

by Dr. Brooks B. Robinson 169

Less Resentment, More Personal

Responsibility, by Karl Miller 200

School Choice Should be a *Right* and

Not a *Want*, by Marie Fischer 211

Blacks Need to be Open to New

Ideas, by John M. Jocelyn 226

Introduction

Richard Showstack

I am registered to vote as a Democrat. In fact, I have always been registered that way since I first signed up to vote. Then I considered myself to be a "Kennedy Democrat," and I still do today.

Kennedy campaigned on the slogan of "getting America moving again." He was in favor of equal rights for African Americans. He also created the Peace Corps, initiated the "space race" which put a man on the moon, advocated on mental health issues, and worked with Congress on affordable housing, equal pay for women, and a host of other agendas.

In the economic arena, JFK is remembered for his tax cuts:

The president finally decided

that only a bold domestic
program, including tax cuts,
would restore his political
momentum. Declaring that
the absence of recession is
not tantamount to economic
growth, the president proposed
in 1963 to cut income taxes
from a range of 20-91% to
14-65% He also proposed
a cut in the corporate tax rate
from 52% to 47%.[1]

In addition:

Kennedy ended a period of tight
fiscal policies, loosening
monetary policy to keep interest
rates down and to encourage

---

[1] https://www.jfklibrary.org/learn/about-jfk/jfk-in-history/john-f-kennedy-on-the-economy-and-taxes

growth of the economy.[2]

In foreign policy:

Kennedy's close advisers
believed that Eisenhower's
foreign policy establishment
was stultified, slow moving,
overly reliant on brinks-
manship and massive
retaliation, and complacent.
Their fear was that after eight
years, the State Department
would be unable to implement
their new international vision.
The new President was deter-
mined to control foreign policy
through a young and energetic
White House and NSC staffers
who would make their own

---

[2] https://en.wikipedia.org/wiki/
John_F._Kennedy#Domestic_policy

informal contacts within the
foreign affairs bureaucracy.[3]

And JFK's brother, Attorney General Robert Kennedy, unleashed an unprecedented war on organized crime.

However, "When liberal Democrats pressed [JFK] to promote progressive social programs, he would often point out that he had not won a mandate and remind them that he first had to be reelected."[4]

Now I know what you are thinking: Kennedy's policies seem more Republican than Democrat, and you're right! What I am trying to say is that the Republican Party today *is the party* of "Kennedy Democrats."

Another thing has changed in the

---

[3] https://history.state.gov/departmenthistory/short-history/jfk-foreignpolicy

[4] https://www.jfklibrary.org/learn/about-jfk/jfk-in-history/john-f-kennedy-on-the-economy-and-taxes

4

Democratic Party: the kind of people who run it. Here were some of the Democratic members of Congress (House and Senate) in the 1960s: Carl Hayden, Sam Rayburn, Mike Mansfield, Carl Albert, J. William Fulbright, Edmund Muskie, Hubert Humphrey, Stuart Symington, William Proxmire, Henry Jackson, Albert Gore, Sr., John Pastore, Wayne Morse, Sam Ervin, Clifford P. Chase, Stuart Udall, James Roosevelt, Daniel Inouye, and George McGovern.

Now I know that, to younger readers, these names mean nothing, but you should know that, whether or not one agreed with them, they were respected (and respectable) men who sincerely wanted to help the country become better. You might even call them "statesmen." They could stand up and tell you their views without attacking their opponents as ignorant fools. They understood what this country stands for and promoted their ideas on which direction it should go.

So who are some of the people who have risen to the top of the Democratic Party today? Joe Biden, Nancy Pelosi, Chuck Shumer, Elizabeth Warren, Maxine Waters, Bernie Sanders, Cory Booker, Kamala Harris, Adam Schiff, Alcee Hastings, Debbie Wasserman Schultz, Rashida Tlaib, Ilhan Omar, Jerry Nadler, Alexandria Ocasio-Cortez, Al Green, Sheila Jackson Lee, Joaquin Castro, Ayanna Pressley, Beto O'Rourke, Kirsten Gillibrand, John Kerry, and Hillary Clinton. None of the people on that list is worthy to carry the briefcase of any of the Democratic members of Congress mentioned above!

The Democrats of the 1960s tower over
them, no doubt looking down on them
in shame and sorrow. In other words,
the Democratic Party today is not
what it was in the past.

The reason for this is that, over the
past 50 years (contrary to what JFK said
in his first Inaugural Speech: "Ask not
what your country can do for you —
ask what you can do for your country."),
the Democrats have adopted a campaign
tactic of saying, "If you vote for us, we
will give you the following things, free
of charge!" In other words, they will
say anything that they think will help
them get (re)elected.

(Note: When I criticize Democrats,
I am criticizing Democratic *elected
officials*, not the misbegotten people
who believe the lies and promises
the Democratic snake oil sellers give

them and then vote for them.)

The problem is that as the Democrats have given more and more government benefits and entitlements to people over the past 50 years, they have had to go further and further to the left to promise even more extreme benefits (free education through college, free health care, free housing and jobs for everyone, etc.). Meanwhile, Progressives in the Education Establishment groom children in elementary school, brainwash them in high school, and propagandize them in college to accept and believe the leftist agenda.

What Has Happened to the Black Community?

When I was a child, my father and brother and I would often attend events at the Los Angeles Coliseum, which was in a black community. Although we were well off, my father was a Depression Era cheapskate who refused to pay the 25 or 30 cents it cost to park next to the Coliseum, so we would park on a street a few blocks away. Were we afraid when, after the event ended in the late evening, we would have to walk a few blocks in the black community to our cars? Sure, but no more afraid than if we would have been walking in any strange community after dark. Would a father be equally willing to walk with his two children through an inner-city black community after dark today? Not likely.

Although I am white, I am very upset about what has happened to the black family and black community over the past 50 years. But rather than blaming white supremacy, institutional racism, unequal education, etc., as the Mainstream Media do, I place the blame squarely on the shoulders of white liberals and the Democratic Party.

I believe that the Democratic Party needs the black vote, and to keep it they (and their minions in the media and the education establishment) have done everything they can to keep blacks on the "plantation" of the Democratic Party by keeping them dependent and angry and afraid to leave. The Democratic Party uses a combination of bribery (through welfare payments and entitlements) and fear to keep blacks on their "plantation." Welfare, entitlements and other special benefits are like a drug to the black community and the Democratic Party (and their enablers) are the drug dealers!

How the Media Help Keep Blacks on the Democratic Party Plantation

The *LA Times*, *Washington Post* and *New York Times* print articles almost daily about how racist America is and how blacks are victims of that racism. They do this for three reasons:

1) To make white liberals feel good about themselves because they are not racists (despite the fact that they never actually do anything or make any sacrifices for needy blacks). (When Clinton was president, someone said that he "made it all right to feel good about yourself even though you don't do any good.")

2) To reinforce the idea that the problems of blacks now are due to "400 years of structural racism" in American society (In 2019, the New York Times published an extensive report claiming that America society has been based on racism since all the way back to 1619.), thus encouraging blacks to blame others for their problems rather than take

responsibility for them.

3) To remind blacks on a daily basis that they are under attack and their only savior is the Democratic Party.

"House Negroes"

Malcolm X spoke about the "house Negro" this way:

> If someone came to the house
> Negro and said, 'Let's go, let's
> separate,' naturally that Uncle
> Tom would say, 'Go where?
> What could I do without boss?
> Where would I live? How would
> I dress? Who would look out for
> me?' That's the house Negro.

But I believe that now the "house negroes" are those blacks (such as Al Sharpton and just about any black who is a host or a guest on CNN or MSNBC) who benefit by echoing the white liberal establishment's mantra of warning blacks, "If you leave the Democratic Party (plantation), who would look out for you?"

Other Groups Have Made It

Other groups have been able to "overcome" the supposed racism of American society. Here are three examples.

First example:

All four of my grandparents emigrated to this country around the year 1900 with nothing more than the clothes they were wearing. Both of my parents' families were dirt poor when they were growing up in the 1910s and 1920s, before welfare, before the New Deal, before civils rights laws, before food stamps and the "War on Poverty."

My father's mother died when my father was a child and his father was a housepainter. My father told us a story

about how he sometimes had to go over
to a relative's house and beg to be given
a potato so his own family would have
something to eat for dinner. My mother's
mother also died when my mother was
young and her father, a shoe repairman,
could not work and take care of four
children at the same time (Aid to
Families with Dependent Children
[AFDC]) was not instituted until 1935),
so my mother and her three brothers
were raised in an orphanage.

Despite this, my father and his two
brothers and my mother and her three
brothers all managed to come to live
middle-class or upper-middle-class lives
as adults. (And they grew up when there
were quotas for Jewish students admitted
to the top American colleges — not
quotas for a *minimum number* of Jews
who could be admitted but for *the*

maximum number of Jews who could be admitted!) None of them ever used illegal drugs or was arrested for anything.

How were they able to be so successful when they were born with about ten strikes against them? I think it was due to their being born into intact families (and extended families) that placed a value on respect, discipline, work, education and their (Jewish) religion and heritage.

A second example:

In the mid-1980s I happened to be walking down the hall past the engineering department at a major university in Southern California. On the wall in front of the department was a list of the names of the students in the department. I was surprised to see more than a dozen names of Vietnamese students on the list.

When I was growing up, I never even knew that there was a country called "Vietnam" until the United States got involved in war there in the mid-1960s. Eventually, of course, the U.S. left Vietnam in defeat in 1975, and that was followed by thousands of "boat people" giving up everything they had to escape the new communist regime of the victors in the war. In the late 1970s, pictures of the escapees in relocation camps outside Vietnam were frequently shown in the media. Luckily for them (and for us), many them were granted entry into the U.S.

So how was it that in the mid-1980s when I saw the list of engineering students on the wall, so many of them were Vietnamese (who must have come to the U.S. when they were 10 to 12 years old not speaking a word of English and whose families had nothing when they arrived)?

The answer, one again, is that they came from strong extended families with a cultural background that emphasized discipline, respect, education and hard work. (I have read stories of "boat people" emigrants who sacrificed and worked 60 to 80 hours a week, or more, to provide a better life for their children.)

A third example:

Much of the recent growth in the foreign-born black population has been fueled by African migration. Between 2000 and 2016, the black African immigrant population more than doubled, from 574,000 to 1.6 million. Africans now make up 39% of the overall foreign-born black

population, up from 24% in
2000. Still, roughly half of all
foreign-born blacks living in
the U.S. in 2016 (49%) were
from the Caribbean, with
Jamaica and Haiti being the
largest source countries.[5]

Blacks who emigrate to this country
from other countries are
indistinguishable (visually) from blacks
who are descended from slaves, and yet
statistics show that black emigrants do
much better than the latter group.

West Indian immigrants to the
United States fare better than
native-born African Americans
on a wide array of economic
measures, including labor force

---

[5] Source: https://www.pewresearch.org/fact-
tank/2018/01/24/key-facts-about-black-
immigrants-in-the-u-s/

participation, earnings, and occupational prestige. Some researchers argue that the root of this difference lies in differing cultural attitudes toward work, while others maintain that white Americans favor West Indian blacks over African Americans, giving them an edge in the workforce. Still others hold that West Indians who emigrate to this country are more ambitious and talented than those they left behind.[6]

And in a letter to the *Wall Street Journal* (Sept. 9, 2019), Karl Miller (a contributor to this book) wrote:

---

[6]https://www.researchgate.net/publication/28728
6340_West_Indian_immigrants_A_black_succe
ss_story

Many studies show that
African-American immigrants
from countries which also had
slavery have also had higher
rates of entrepreneurship and
higher educational achievement
when they moved here than
African-Americans born in
America, despite the latter
having access to many social
and affirmative-action
programs. Many immigrants
of all colors have experienced
hardships in their former
countries which few born in
America in the last 60 years
ever have.

So Why Haven't Blacks Been Able to "Overcome" like Other Groups?

So why haven't blacks done as well as these examples over the past 50 years? Why haven't they been able to "overcome" their circumstances and situation?

People cite three possible reasons for the disparities between white and black achievement:

1) the legacy of 400 years of institutional racism

"The legacy of slavery and segregation and Jim Crow and suppression is alive and well in every aspect of the economy and in the country." (Beto O'Rourke in the June 30, 2019, Democratic candidates debate)

But by many measures, black communities were doing *better* 75 years ago than they are doing now. If their problems are due to "the legacy of 400 years of institutional racism," is this legacy *worse* now than it was in the past?

2) America is still racist.

Yes, there are racists in America (and there will always be), but America is the least racist it has ever been and it has done more to fight racism than any other nation in the world. And how do you explain the vast numbers of blacks who have succeeded despite whatever racism exists (or the vast number of non-white people risking their lives to enter this country illegally)?

And some people believe:

3) Blacks are genetically inferior or just too stupid to catch up.

But I don't believe that for a second! There are too many examples of brilliant blacks (and white idiots!) for that to be true.

However, in my opinion, there are four other phenomena that have contributed more than anything else to the lack of progress in the black community over the past 50 years:

1) The "Soft Bigotry of Low Expectations"

This refers to having "low expectations" of minorities in schools or other areas of achievement, and it is considered a form of bigotry.

According to Holly Kuzmich:

A recent study by Seth Gershenson of American University and Nicholas Papageorge of Johns Hopkins University followed students who were in 10th grade in 2002 through to 2012. They found that white teachers on average had significantly

lower expectations for black
students than they did for
white students.

The study also showed that
those lower expectations
impact achievement; having
teachers who were confident
that their students would
complete college made a real
difference in their college
attainment.[7]

And in 2018, Dr. Terry Stoops wrote:

As he campaigned for the Republican
presidential nomination in the winter of
1999, then-Gov. George W. Bush
delivered his memorable "soft bigotry
of low expectations" speech before the
Latino Business Association in Los

[7] https://www.the74million.org/article/the-soft-bigotry-of-low-expectations-still-alive-and-well-16-years-later-an-insider-looks-back-at-the-legacy-of-no-child-left-behind/

Angeles.

"Now some say it is unfair to hold disadvantaged children to rigorous standards," Bush remarked. "I say it is discrimination to require anything less — the soft bigotry of low expectations." The phrase... captures well the widespread indifference toward the persistently appalling academic performance of African-American and Latino students in our nation's public schools.

Nearly 18 years after Bush first uttered the phrase, little has changed.

After North Carolina education officials released the 2017-18 accountability and test results in early September, few North Carolinians bemoaned the abysmal performance of disadvantaged children, particularly African-American males, on state standardized reading tests. Even fewer voiced outrage at the generations of disadvantaged children that have been ill-served by our public schools. The organizations and activists who claim to be the moral conscience of the state chose instead to score political points by criticizing the state's sizable investment in Read to Achieve, a well-intentioned initiative established by the Republican-led General Assembly in 2012 to ensure that all public school children read at grade level by third grade.

Of course, those critics failed to acknowledge that Read to Achieve is simply the latest in a series of multimillion-dollar programs that have failed to improve literacy for public school students. Before the election of a Republican legislative majority, Democrats concocted various plans to address the problem.... In other words, neither Democrats nor Republicans have improved literacy instruction for our most vulnerable populations, and state test scores bear that out.

Last year, 57.3 percent of students in grades three through eight were proficient in reading, a mere 1 percentage point improvement since 2014. Of course, statewide figures obscure the performance of student racial and ethnic subgroups. Only around 40 percent of black elementary and middle-schoolers reached grade-level reading proficiency. Far fewer earned scores that reach levels of achievement that ensure college and career readiness.

Further disaggregated data reveal even more disconcerting facts about reading achievement in North Carolina. Statewide, around one-third of black males in the state read at grade level last year, and under one-fourth reached the higher career and college ready level of performance. Only three subgroups — students with disabilities, English language learners, and homeless students — had lower levels of reading proficiency. At least four out of five black male students failed to reach reading proficiency at nearly 200 public elementary and middle schools across the state. A handful of these schools had single-digit reading proficiency rates for black males.[8]

---

[8] https://www.carolinajournal.com/opinion-article/overcoming-the-soft-bigotry-of-low-expectations-for-black-males/

But who has lower expectations for blacks, Democrats (who believe blacks can't make it without their help) or Republicans (who believe that blacks can be just as successful as any other group if only the government would stop "helping" them and subsidizing their "victocrat" mentality)?

Radio talk show host Larry Elder coined this term.

> A "victocrat" is a person who has attached a political methodology to the condition of being a victim. Usually, the victim is not really a victim at all, or at least not nearly as much of a victim as the victocrats wine and complain. Typical victims which are used by victocrats to push a liberal political agenda are: minorities, women,

children, the working poor,
unmarried mothers, animals...
even the environment.[9]

Remember: The more you subsidize something, the more of it you get; the more you tax something, the less of it you get.

A second reason is:

2) the increased rate of black single women giving birth

Now three-quarters of black babies are born to a single mother who may not be well-educated herself. Plus, they are born in poor areas where they grow up with a lack of positive male role models and the discipline meted out by their fathers.

Let's take a look, for example, at what has happened to the rate of black unmarried women giving birth since

---

[9] https://answers.yahoo.com/question/index?qid=20080818205609AAxulWB

the "War on Poverty" began.

You can see in the chart below that in 1930-1934, 31% of (first-born) babies born to black women were born before the mother's marriage, and that number remained fairly through 1964.

Years	Percent of Births Before Marriage
1990-94	76.9
1985-89	73.3
1980-84	71.2
1975-79	67.4
1970-74	59.0
1965-69	53.6
1960-64	36.1
1955-59	40.9
1950-54	32.6
1945-49	32.2
1940-44	27.5
1935-39	37.9
1930-34	31.0

[Source: https://www.census.gov/prod/99pubs/p23-197.pdf]

But looked what happened starting in 1964 (the year the so-called "War on Poverty" began). It skyrocketed, and by 1990 the rate had risen to 64 percent for black infants.[10]

Here is a chart that shows rate of births to unmarried black — and other — women (ages 15-44) from 1952 to 2007):

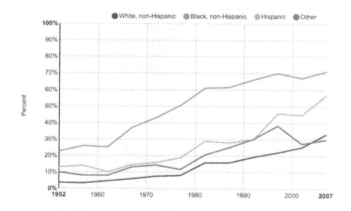

[Source: https://ifstudies.org/blog/ trends-in-unmarried-childbearing- point-to-a-coming-apart]

---

[10] https://www.brookings.edu/research/an-analysis-of-out-of-wedlock-births-in-the-united-states/ point-to-a-coming-apart

31

Once again, as you can see, the rate was relatively stable until it started to skyrocket in the late 1960s.

Here is a figure that shows the percent of all births to unmarried women by race in 1980, 1990 and 1999.

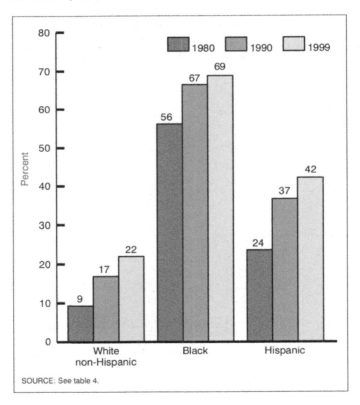

[Source: https://www.cdc.gov/nchs/
data/nvsr/nvsr48/nvs48_16.pdf]

The percentage of births to unmarried black women was 57% in 1980. By 1990 it was 64%, and in 2000, it was about 69%.[11]

According to a 2015 federal study, "More than three quarters of African American births [were] to unmarried women, nearly double the illegitimacy rate of all other births."[12]

Since 2008, more than six million black children have been in single-parent households.[13]

Of course, the rate of out-of-wedlock births has been going up for all sectors of

[11] https://www.childtrends.org/wp-content/uploads/2015/03/75_Births_to_Unmarried_Women.pdf
[12] https://www.washingtonexaminer.com/77-black-births-to-single-moms-49-for-hispanic-immigrants
[13] https://www.brookings.edu/research/an-analysis-of-out-of-wedlock-births-in-the-united-states/

American society since the 1960s, but the black community has been hit hardest.

And according to Brookings, "[F]or children living in single-parent homes, the odds of living in poverty are great. The policy implications of the increase in out-of-wedlock births are staggering."[14]

And which party has been advocating for "family values" and responsible behavior, and which party doesn't care how you act as long as you vote for them?

3) Democrats Run the Big Cities

A third factor that blacks have to overcome is that most blacks are born and raised in big cities which are run by the Democratic Party.

---

[14] https://www.brookings.edu/research/an-analysis-of-out-of-wedlock-births-in-the-united-states/

But aren't Democrats the "party of the people" (the poor, racial and other kinds of minorities)? Haven't the Democrats' policies helped the black community over the past 50 years?

Let's take a look at what a good job Democrats are doing in running cities which they are in charge of, such as how well they are doing at fighting crime:

U.S. Cities with Highest Crime Rates (in alphabetical order)	Political Party of the Mayor
Albuquerque, NM	Dem
Atlanta, GA	Dem
Baltimore, MD	Dem
Birmingham, AL	Dem
Buffalo, NY	Dem
Chicago, IL	Dem
Cleveland, OH	Dem
Detroit, MI	Dem
Indianapolis, IN	Dem
Kansas City, MO	Dem
Lansing, MI	Dem
Little Rock, AR	Dem

Memphis, TN	Dem
Milwaukee, WI	Dem
Minneapolis, NY	Dem
Nashville, IL	Dem
Oakland, CA	Dem
Rockford, IL	Dem
Springfield, Il	Dem
Springfield, MO	Dem
St. Louis, MO	Dem
Stockton, CA	Dem
Toledo, OH	Dem
Washington, DC	Dem

[Source: https://www.cbsnews.com/
pictures/murder-map-deadliest-u-s-cities/6/]

And how well have Democratic city governments done at combatting the scourge of "income inequality"?

The 10 Cities with the *Highest* Income Inequality	Political Party of the City's Mayor
1. Bridgeport, CT	Democrat
2. New York, NY	Democrat
3. San Francisco, CA	Democrat
4. Los Angeles, CA	Democrat

5. New Orleans, LA	Democrat
6. San Jose, CA	Democrat
7. Miami, FL	Republican
8. Houston, TX	Democrat
9. Fresno, CA	Republican
10. Boston, MA	Democrat

[Source: https://www.brookings.edu/research/
city-and-metropolitan-income-inequality-
data-reveal-ups-and-downs-through-2016/]

And what about dealing with the

homeless?

U.S. Cities with the *Most* Homeless People (in alphabetical order)	Political Party of the Mayor
Boston	Dem
Chicago	Dem
District of Columbia	Dem
Honolulu	Dem
Las Vegas	Dem
Los Angeles	Dem
New York City	Dem
Philadelphia	Dem
Phoenix	Dem
Portland	Dem
San Diego	Rep
San Francisco	Dem

San Jose/ Santa Clara, CA	Dem
Seattle	Dem

[Source: https://www.ranker.com/list/top-10-u-s-cities-with-a-high-homelessness-rate/greg]

Finally, here are the results of research by Orkin Pest Control:

Cities with the Worst Rat Problems*	Political Party of the Mayor
1. Chicago	Dem
2. Los Angeles	Dem
3. New York	Dem
4. Washington, DC	Dem
5. San Francisco	Dem
6. Detroit	Dem
7. Philadelphia	Dem
8. Cleveland	Dem
9. Baltimore	Dem
10. Denver	Dem
11. Minneapolis-St. Paul	Dem
12. Dallas/Ft. Worth	Dem
13. Boston	Dem
14. Seattle	Dem
15. Atlanta	Dem
16. Indianapolis	Dem
17. Miami-Ft. Lauderdale	Rep
18. Hartford	Dem

19. Pittsburgh	Dem
20. Cincinnati	Dem
21. Milwaukee	Dem
22. Charlotte	Dem
23. Houston	Dem
24. Portland	Dem
25. Columbus	Dem

* Not including Democratic politicians

[Source: http://mentalfloss.com/article/561029/
most-rat-infested-cities-in-america]

And how are the education systems in cities run by Democrats?

U.S. Cities with the Lowest Educational Achievement Scores (in alphabetical order)	Political Party of the Mayor
Albuquerque, NM	Dem
Atlanta, GA	Dem
Bakersfield, CA	Rep
Baltimore, MD	Dem
Chicago	Dem
Cleveland, OH	Dem
Dallas, TX	Dem
Denver, CO	Dem
Detroit, MI	Dem
District of Columbia	Dem
Fort Worth, TX	Rep
Fresno, CA	Rep
Houston, TX	Dem
Las Vegas, NV	Dem

Los Angeles, CA	Dem
Milwaukee, WI	Dem
Modesto, CA	Rep
New York City	Dem
Ocala, Fla.	Rep
Philadelphia, PA	Dem
Stockton-Lodi, CA	Dem

[Source: https://en.wikipedia.org/wiki/
List_of_U.S._states_and_territories_
by_educational_attainment]

And how have young blacks fared
in the teachers-union-run schools in
the Democratic-Party-run big cities?
Not well:

> African American students
> are often located in schools
> with less qualified teachers,
> teachers with lower salaries
> and novice teachers....
>
> African American students
> are less likely to be college-
> ready. In fact, 61 percent of
> ACT-tested black students in
> the 2015 high school
> graduating class met none
> of the four ACT college

readiness benchmarks, nearly twice the 31 percent rate for all students....

In 2015, the average reading score for white students on the National Assessment of Educational Progress (NAEP) 4th and 8th grade exam was 26 points higher than black students. Similar gaps are apparent in math. The 12th grade assessment also show alarming disparities as well, with only seven percent of black students performing at or above proficient on the math exam in 2015, compared to 32 percent white students.[15]

As Walter E. Williams wrote, several years ago:

Project Baltimore began an investigation of Baltimore's

---

[15] https://www.uncf.org/pages/k-12-disparity-facts-and-stats

school system. What they found was an utter disgrace. In 19 of Baltimore's high schools, out of 3,804 students, only 14 of them, or less than 1%, were proficient in math. In 13 of Baltimore's 39 high schools, not a single student scored proficient in math. In five Baltimore City high schools, not a single student scored proficient in math or reading. Despite these academic deficiencies, about 70% of the students graduate and are conferred a high school diploma. A high school diploma attests that the holder can read, write and compute at a 12th-grade level. Obviously, the diplomas conferred on students who have not mastered reading, writing and computing are fraudulent....

Dr. Thomas Sowell's research in *Education: Assumptions Versus History* documents academic excellence at Baltimore's Frederick Douglass High School and others. This academic excellence occurred during an era when blacks were much poorer and faced gross racial discrimination. It's worthwhile reading for black people to learn the capabilities of other blacks facing so many challenging circumstances. I'm wondering when the black community will demand an end to an educational environment that condemns so many youngsters to mediocrity.[16]

---

[16]

https://townhall.com/columnists/walterewilliams/2019/09/18/racist-exam-questions-n2553173

One More Handicap: The "War on Poverty"

However, there is one more handicap that blacks have had to overcome:

4) They have grown up under the paternalistic policies of the "War on Poverty," whose underlying assumption is that blacks can't make it without the help of government. This tends to make them feel like "victocrats" who are helpless to solve their own problems. This, in turn, has led to a loss of personal responsibility and the self-destructive behavior rampant in poor black communities. The country's emphasis on welfare with little or no emphasis on personal responsibility has also led to the present situation where more than 75% of black women are "married" to the federal government and more than one-third of black men have felony

convictions[17] (in 1980, it was 13%[18])
and by age 23, nearly 50 percent of
America's black males have been
arrested.[19]

But haven't the Democrats helped
lift blacks out of poverty through their
"War on Poverty," and various social
programs? Let's look at the facts.

According to two 2013 articles
in the (liberal) Washington Post:

> Black poverty fell quickly
> between 1959 and 1969, from
> 55.1 percent to 32.2 percent. But
> after that, the drop was slower
> and more uneven. In 2011, 27.6
> percent of black households

---

[17] https://www.sentencingproject.org/news/5593/
[18] https://www.ncbi.nlm.nih.gov/pmc/
articles/PMC5996985/
[19] https://www.citylab.com/equity/2014/01/
nearly-50-percent-black-males-have-been-
arrested-age-23/8042/

were in poverty — nearly triple
the poverty rate for whites.

And:

Fifty years ago, the
unemployment rate was 5
percent for whites and 10.9
percent for blacks, according to
the Economic Policy Institute.
Today, it is 6.6 percent for
whites and 12.6 percent for
blacks. Over the past 30 years,
the average white family has
gone from having five times as
much wealth as the average
black family to 61 / 2 times,
according to the Urban Institute.

And according to the Economic
Policy Institute:

Black poverty, as with poverty
overall, declined dramatically
through the 1960s, falling from

a rate of 55.1 percent in 1959 to 32.2 percent in 1969. Since then, progress in reducing black poverty has been agonizingly slow and uneven. By 1989 the black poverty rate had only declined to 30.7 percent.[20]

And the Washington Post notes, "Both white and black poverty fell dramatically during the 1960s, though the drop in black poverty from 55.1 percent in 1959 to 32.2 percent in 1969 is particularly remarkable."[21]

Remember, this "remarkable" drop in black poverty began *before* the "War on Poverty" fully took effect.

Look at this chart (from the "Number

---

[20] https://www.epi.org/publication/unfinished-march-overview/

[21] https://www.washingtonpost.com/news/wonk/wp/2012/07/11/poverty-in-the-50-years-since-the-other-america-in-five-charts

of Families Below the Poverty Level
and Poverty Rate: 1959 to 2017):

Notice how much the poverty rate
was already going down *before* the
"War on Poverty" took effect:

Year	In 1000's	%
1959	8,320	18.5
1960	8,243	18.1
1961	8,391	18.1
1962	8,077	17.2
1963	7,554	15.9
1964	7,160	15.0
1965	6,721	13.9
1966	5,784	11.8

[Source: U.S. Bureau of the Census,
Current Population Survey, Annual
Social and Economic Supplements.]

And the chart also shows that, despite
the "War on Poverty," the poverty rate
for families *has remained "remarkably" unchanged* since 1966.

But what about the poverty rate for
blacks specifically? Take a look at this
chart.

Year	Percent in Poverty
2017	22.7
2016	22.7
2015	23.2
2014	23.1
2013	22.0
2013	24.4
2012	23.5
2011	23.6
2010	23.2
2009	22.8
2008	23.5
2007	24.8
2006	24.8
2005	24.8
2004	24.3
2003	24.5
2002	24.9
2001	24.7
2000	25.3
1999	25.7
1998	26.4
1997	25.6
1996	26.5
1995	27.1
1994	26.8
1993	27.7
1992	28.5
1991	28.7
1990	29.3
1989	29.5
1988	29.5
1987	29.5
1986	27.8
1985	27.0
1984	28.2
1983	28.0
1982	28.2
1981	28.8
1980	29.3
1979	30.9
1978	31.1
1977	31.3
1976	30.4
1975	29.2
1974	30.7
1973	32.2
1972	31.5
1971	28.9
1970	29.7
1969	29.4

[Source: U.S. Bureau of the Census, Current Population Survey, Annual Social and Economic Supplements.]

As you can see, despite the "War on Poverty," the black poverty rate did not start to decline significantly until the "Dot-Com Boom" of the 1990's, and it has remained steady for the past ten years. (And remember that, according to the previous chart, the overall poverty rate had already been declining significantly between 1959 and 1966.)

And, perhaps most damning of all, the ratio of black unemployment to the white unemployment rate has also remained "remarkably" constant:

Ratio of black to white unemployment rate, 1963–2012

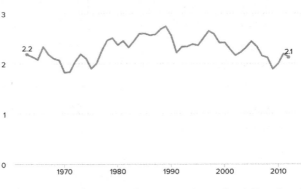

[Source: https://www.epi.org/publication/ unfinished-march-overview/]

Affirmative Action

But don't blacks need help to overcome the "400 years of institutional racism" of American society? What about some form of "affirmative action"? According to the Heritage Foundation:

> [O]ne of the unintended consequences of these affirmative action policies [is that s]tudents admitted based on their skin color, rather than their merit, may end up "mismatched" with their school, which leads to low grades and high dropout rates....
>
> Affirmative action-induced low grades are a serious problem....
> For example, in one study of top law schools, more than 50 percent of African-American law students (many of whom had been admitted pursuant to affirmative action policies) were in the bottom 10 percent of their class. And the dropout rate among African-American students was more than twice that of their white peers (19.3 percent vs. 8.2 percent)....

The problem doesn't stop there. Because of affirmative action policies, fewer minorities enter careers in science, technology, engineering, and math (STEM) fields. This is not due to a lack of talented minority students — of which there are many....

Neither is it due to a lack of interest. Study after study shows that minorities tend to be more interested in STEM fields than their white counterparts. But admitting students with lower high school grades and SAT math scores into schools with elite science and math programs is a recipe for disaster....

Thus, students should be encouraged to apply to universities where their credentials are matched with those of their fellow students. Merit-based admissions are a "win-win" situation. Students end up at institutions where they are more likely to graduate and in the field of study they actually want to pursue.[22]

---

[22] https://www.heritage.org/courts/commentary/

So, has the "War on Poverty" succeeded? Again, according to the Heritage Foundation:

> In his January 1964 State of the Union address, [Lyndon] Johnson proclaimed, "This administration today, here and now, declares unconditional war on poverty in America. Since that time, U.S. taxpayers have spent over $22 trillion on anti-poverty programs (in constant 2012 dollars). Adjusted for inflation, this spending (which does not include Social Security or Medicare) is three times the cost of all military wars in

---

how-affirmative-action-colleges-hurts-minority-students

U.S. history since the
American Revolution.
Despite this mountain of
spending, progress against
poverty, at least as measured
by the government, has
been minimal.

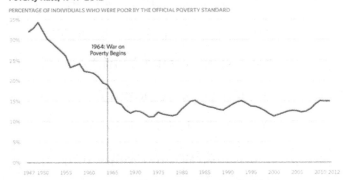

Poverty Rate, 1947–2012

PERCENTAGE OF INDIVIDUALS WHO WERE POOR BY THE OFFICIAL POVERTY STANDARD

Sources: Figures for 1947-1958: Gordon Fisher, "Estimates of the Poverty Population Under the Current Official Definition for Years Before 1959," U.S. Department of Health and Human Services, Office of the Assistant Secretary for Planning and Evaluation, 1986. Figures for 1959-2012: U.S. Census Bureau, Current Population Survey, Annual Social and Economic Supplements, "Historical Poverty Tables—People," Table 2, https://www.census.gov/hhes/www/poverty/data/historical/people.html (accessed September 10, 2014).

[Source: https://www.heritage.org/poverty-and-
inequality/report/the-war-poverty-after-50-
years]

And, finally:

With respect to homeownership,
unemployment, and incarceration,
America has failed to deliver any
progress for African Americans over
the last five decades. In these areas,
their situation has either failed to
improve relative to whites or has
worsened. In 2017 the black
unemployment rate was 7.5 percent,
up from 6.7 percent in 1968, and is
still roughly twice the white
unemployment rate. In 2015, the
black homeownership rate was just
over 40 percent, virtually unchanged
since 1968, and trailing a full 30
points behind the white
homeownership rate, which saw
modest gains over the same period.
And the share of African Americans
in prison or jail almost tripled
between 1968 and 2016 and is
currently more than six times the
white incarceration rate.[23]

[23] https://www.epi.org/publication/50-years-after-the-kerner-commission/

As the old joke goes, "We fought a war on poverty and poverty won!"

There's another old saying: "Insanity is doing the same thing over and over and expecting to get a different result." We're spent 50 years and tens of trillions of dollars trying to end poverty using the Democrats' way of doing. Isn't it time to try something else?

Please stop helping us!

There used to be a joke that if someone said to you, "I'm from the government and I'm here to help you," you should turn and run away.

In fact, in the Introduction to Jason Riley's 2014 book, *Please Stop Helping Us: How Liberals Make It Harder for Blacks to Succeed*, he writes about "the political left's serial altruism over the past half century":

What if there are limits to what government can do beyond removing barriers to freedom? What if the best that we can hope for from our elected officials are policies that promote equal opportunity? What if public-policy makers risk creating more barriers to progress when the goal is the ever-elusive "equality as a result"? At what point does helping start hurting?...

Have popular government policies and programs that are aimed at helping blacks worked as intended? And where black advancement has occurred, do these government efforts deserve the credit that they so often receive? The intentions behind welfare programs, for example, may be noble. But in practice they have slowed the self-development that proved necessary for other groups to advance. Minimum-wage laws might lift earnings for people who are already employed, but they also have a long history of pricing blacks out of the labor force. Affirmative action in higher education was intended to address past discrimination, but the result is fewer

black college graduates—particularly
in the fields of math and science—
than we'd have in the absence of racial
preferences. And so it goes, with
everything from soft-on-crime laws
that make black neighborhoods more
dangerous to policies that limit school
choice out of a mistaken belief that
charter schools and voucher programs
harm the traditional public schools that
most low-income students attend.

In theory, these efforts are meant to
help. In practice, they become barriers to
moving forward.... time and again the
empirical data show that current methods
and approaches have come up short.
Upward mobility depends on work and
family. Social programs that undermine
the work ethic and displace fathers keep
poor people poor, and perverse
incentives put in place by people trying
to help are manifested in black attitudes,
habits, and skills. Why study hard in
school if you will be held to lower
academic standards? Why change
antisocial behavior when people are
willing to reward it, make excuses for it,

or even change the law to accommodate it?

I hope that you are beginning to realize that, whatever good intentions they may have had, social welfare programs promoted by the Democratic have done more harm than good to the black community.

Jason Riley says this about that:

The left's sentimental support has turned underprivileged blacks into playthings for liberal intellectuals and politicians who care more about clearing their conscience or winning votes than advocating behaviors and attitudes that have allowed other groups to get ahead....

There is no question that the civil rights lobby has benefited tremendously from the programs launched by the Great Society. So has a Democratic Party that rewards black constituents with government handouts.

In fact, one might argue (as I have) that the white liberals of the Democratic Party care more about the welfare of their party than the welfare of their black constituents.

As Tammy Bruce wrote:

> While some Democratic leaders insist it's America's 400 years of racism that's responsible for the condition of inner cities, it is instead a systemic addiction to power and money that is ravaging Democratic-run metropolises and continues unabated because the Democratic Party doesn't actually care about people's lives, simply seeing them as fodder in their political wars.[24]

---

[24]

https://www.washingtontimes.com/news/2019/aug/1/how-democrats-destroyed-baltimore-and-other-americ/?fbclid=IwAR0d45WcjiRER_lJ-

"Institutional Racism"

Is "institutional racism" really the biggest problem that blacks now face? Dennis Prager wrote:

> ABC News correspondent Linsey Davis: "I'd like to start with young black voters. Several recent polls indicate their No. 1 concern is racism."
>
> Nothing more clearly divides left from right than this statement. The left says the No. 1 problem facing black Americans is racism. No one else does. Anyone who says racism is a greater problem than, for example, the absence of black fathers (more than three-quarters of black children are born to unwed mothers) either is woefully ignorant or purposefully wants to spread racial division.
>
> Furthermore, if such polls exist and they are right, there is no hope for black America in this generation. It means that

---

GCsARmgCi0TqO5eHSj5pf92JosBEmqntQJJO
iyrUic

the left has successfully indoctrinated young Americans, white and black, into believing that a truly decent country is so indecent it hates its black population.[25]

Geoffrey Moore wrote:

Black America has a growing problem that needs to be addressed. It is, in my opinion, the most persistent problem facing us as a race in this country. Despite what "our" media-appointed black leaders tell us, this problem is not racism, reparations, affirmative action, President Bush or the Confederate Battle Flag. It's attitude.

Overall, we have terrible attitudes. If we want our situation to change, our attitudes will have to lead the way. Many of our so-called leaders would like us to believe that we as individuals have absolutely no control over our lives. They want us to think that the only way blacks will escape from our predicament

---

[25]

https://townhall.com/columnists/dennisprager/2019/09/17/do-you-know-what-the-democrats-said-at-their-debate-n2553194

is to continue to support them and let them maintain their bases of power. It's in their financial interest that we continue to view ourselves as powerless victims....

We all have the power and ability to take control of our lives and indeed make it.[26]

Looking forward to the 2020 presidential election, Patrick Gavaghan Muth wrote in the *Baltimore Sun*:

What has made our nation the envy of the world is not the assurance of happiness as Ms. Warren and Mr. Sanders might have us believe, but the protection of its pursuit. This is an oft-overlooked yet critical distinction. While candidates rage about the "evil" drug companies and corporate over-lords (about some of which they are undoubtedly correct), they promulgate,

---

[26] https://nationalcenter.org/project21/2004/01/01/how-to-make-it-in-america-by-geoffrey-moore/

intentionally or otherwise, what's come to be known as the soft bigotry of low expectations. Yes, we need to address unsustainable income inequality, the lack of access to quality health care for all Americans and the impending automation of millions of more jobs. But we need to do so via partnerships with government, corporations, non-profits, and an electorate that is not condescendingly told they are incapable of achieving happiness without dictates from on high. Where is the call for the categorically American ideal of self-determination that defined JFK's Democratic legacy? "Ask not what your country can do for you; ask what you can do for your country" is seemingly antithetical to many in the post-Trump Democratic Party.[27]

---

[27] https://www.baltimoresun.com/opinion/op-ed/bs-ed-op-0708-trumpian-dems-20190702-story.html

Remember: It would be a disaster for the Democratic Party if blacks escaped the Democratic Planation and started to do well because, if they did so, why would they need the "plantation owners" in the Democratic Party? So, it is to the advantage of the Democratic Party to keep blacks ignorant, afraid, angry, and dependent and to continue blaming white racism for their plight. Once blacks realize that they have been brainwashed and used and lied to and played by the Democratic Party, that will be the end of that party as we know it.

The Facts Don't Lie

So why doesn't anyone publicly acknowledge the facts listed above and point at the Democratic Party as the culprit. The answer is that if a black person does so he is called an "Uncle Tom," and if a white person does so he is called a racist. And if a black person dares to suggest that the Democratic Party (or the NCAAP) is not really the friend of black people, he is called a "race traitor" or "self-hating black."

As Ben Carson said:

> In our society, for some people on the other side, the only thing worse than Satan is a black conservative.... Blacks are supposed to think a certain way.... If you do not think that way, you are an Uncle Tom. To me, [you] know what that sounds like? Racism.[28]

However, despite the continuing propaganda of the Liberal-Democrat-

---

[28] https://townhall.com/tipsheet/timothymeads/2019/07/01/ben-carson-lef...ink-the-only-thing-worse-than-satan-is-a-black-conservative-n2549257

Media-Education establishment, a
change is happening:

> The African-American electorate
> has been undergoing a quiet, long-term
> transformation, moving from the left
> toward the center on several social
> and cultural issues, while remaining
> decisively liberal, even radical, on
> economic issues, according to a series
> of studies by prominent African-
> American scholars.
>
> "There has been a shift in the attitudes
> of black masses about the extent to which
> systematic discrimination and prejudice
> are the primary reasons blacks continue
> to lag behind whites," Candis Watts
> Smith, a political scientist at Penn State,
> wrote in a paper published in the Journal
> of Black Studies in 2014, "Shifting From
> Structural to Individual Attributions of

67

Black Disadvantage: Age, Period and Cohort Effects on Black Explanations of Racial Disparities."

Smith argues that older black Americans with deeply ingrained memories of the civil rights struggles of the 1960s and 1970s have been joined by a younger generation, with the result that African Americans' attention has increasingly shifted from structural reasons of black disadvantage (e.g., systematic discrimination in the job or housing markets) to individual-based explanations (e.g., lack of individual motivation; oppositional attitudes to school and learning) of these disparities, especially in the post-civil rights era.[29]

---

[29] https://www.nytimes.com/2019/09/11/opinion/black-voters-democrats-2020-election.html

In Conclusion

I am deeply saddened by the number of blacks (and non-blacks) who have succumbed to the brainwashing campaign by the Democratic Party and believe that Republicans are their enemies, and their overseers, Democrats, are their friends.

But don't just take my word for it. In the following pages, twelve respected blacks explain why they have concluded that it is time for blacks to reconsider their unquestioned (and undeserved) loyalty to the Democratic Party.

Steal Away!

In 1841, Frederick Douglass spoke at
a Boston gathering of the Massachusetts
Anti-Slavery Society:

What should we do with the
Negro? I have had but one
answer from the beginning.
Do nothing with us! Your doing
with us has already played the
mischief with us. Do nothing with
us! If the apples will not remain
on the tree of their own strength,
if they are worm-eaten at the
core, if they are early ripe and
disposed to fall, let them fall....
And if the Negro cannot stand
on his own legs, let him fall also.
All I ask is, give him a chance
 to stand on his own legs!

**Essays on why blacks
should reconsider their allegiance
to the Democratic Party**

*A black Christian conservative
Republican activist and writer,
Lloyd Marcus explains how his
life experiences drove him to
not see himself as a "victim."*

Why Blacks Must
Stop Voting Democrat

Lloyd Marcus

A rabbi on TV said one of the reasons
why Jews have prospered despite being
the most persecuted people on the planet
is ancient Jewish wisdom says to never
view oneself as a victim. This powerful
truth hit me like a ton of bricks. From as
far back as I can remember, Democrats
have deceived blacks by drilling the lie
into their heads that they are victims of
an eternally racist America.

Insidiously, Democrats continue to
sell blacks the lie that America is a

72

hellhole of racism in which Republicans
and Conservatives are obsessed with
conceiving ways to keep blacks down.
Consequently, far too many blacks
absurdly believe a majority of Americans (Trump voters) are white
supremacists and their only hope of
keeping them at bay is to continue
voting for Democrats.

As a child, I instinctively knew
Democrats were scamming blacks.
When I was around nine years old,
my parents and three younger siblings
moved from a leaky roof ghetto to
a new 11-story government project
in Baltimore. Everything (kitchen
appliances and so on) was brand new.
Extremely excited, we were among the
first of the black families in the building.
Within a short amount of time, that
building became a huge ghetto. The

elevators were routinely out-of-service due to vandalism. Our apartment was on the sixth floor. Entering the pitch-black stairwell to walk up to our apartment was like walking into the shadow of death, as the sound of stepping on broken wine bottles echoed off the concrete walls. I suspect my fellow residents were Democrats. Every problem was always the fault of white racism.

At nine years old, I sarcastically said, "How can we stop mean white people from sneaking into our building at night, breaking light bulbs in the stairwells, peeing, breaking the elevators and smashing wine bottles?" Even at that young age, common sense told me "whitey" was not responsible for problems we could fix ourselves.

In my mid-twenties, I again noticed the devastating negative consequences of Democrats infecting blacks with victim mindsets. I became a born-again Christian. Excited about my new life in Jesus, I began visiting reform schools and prisons sharing how Jesus changed my life. Shockingly, a majority of the inmates were young black men. Many were gifted and talented. Their glaring problem was not white racism, but hopeless victim mindsets instilled into them by Democrats. I repeatedly heard, "Why even try when whitey has systemically stacked the deck against you?

Blacks today do not know the Democratic party has become the home of socialists, communists, progressives and anti-Americanism. All Democrats care about is furthering their anti-God agenda. The folks they claim to advocate (minorities, women and LGBTQ) are nothing more than useful idiots. Democrats want blacks to hate their country. This is why Democrats say all black success is *in spite of* America's rabid racism.

Americans are good fair-minded people. This is why white America elected Obama, the first black president, exempting him from the normal vetting process. It is unarguable that white America elected Obama because blacks are only 12% of the population. Hidden by his black skin exterior, Obama was socialists/progressives' perfect Trojan Horse to further their godless and anti-American agenda. White Americans naively assumed electing a black president would finally end them being branded racist. They had no idea that Democrats would exploit Obama's skin color, using it as a bludgeon to force their agenda down the throats of Americans.

Anyone who dared to speak out against any of Obama's numerous unconstitutional executive orders was immediately attacked, high-tech beaten and lynched in the public square, an "R" branded on their forehead for being a racist.

My conservative self-reliant, the-world-does-not-owe-me-anything mindset came from my parents. Particularly, my dad, the late Dr. Rev. Lloyd E Marcus. In 1952, the ban won allowing blacks to take the civil service test was lifted. Dad passed the test and became a Baltimore City firefighter. White firefighters at Engine 6 resented Dad and treated him like scum. Dad was assigned separate eating utensils, restroom and sleeping area. He could not even pour himself a cup of coffee from the same coffeepot as the whites.

But Dad was the young assistant pastor of a Baltimore storefront church. Whenever the humiliation become too overwhelming, Dad retreated to the storage room to pray and read his Bible. Mean-spirited firefighters named the storage room, "Marcus' Chapel." Dad courageously endured because he had a wife and four kids to feed and knew he was a trailblazer.

Rather than wallowing in a victim mindset, Dad chose to represent Jesus by striving to be excellent. Dad won "Firefighter of the Year" two times, also winning respect and lifelong friendships with white firefighters. (Dad competed with whites for Firefighter of the Year without Democrats' insulting demands that standards be lowered to compensate for his skin color.) He went on to became

Baltimore's first black paramedic and fire department chaplain.

I hate that Democrats always send blacks the message that they are inferior to whites, repeatedly demanding lowered standards and special concessions. For example: Democrats say requiring blacks to present a photo ID to vote disenfranchises them. This is extremely insulting. In essence, Democrats are saying that, unlike other Americans, blacks are too stupid to acquire a photo ID, which is absurd. You need a photo ID to cash a check, board an airplane and countless other transactions. And yet, far too many blacks view this attack on their intelligence as Democrats advocating for them.

The true evil goal of Democrats is not to empower blacks. Their real goal is to addict blacks to government dependency.

Why? Because if the government is paying your bills, the government can totally control your life, dictating your behavior. This is why Democrats despise self-reliant extraordinarily successful blacks like Supreme Court Justice Clarence Thomas, Secretary of Housing and Urban Development Dr. Ben Carson, former Secretary of State Condoleezza Rice and businessman extraordinaire Herman Cain. The success of these blacks punches a huge hole in Democrats' lie that blacks are eternal victims of racist America.

Tragically, blacks have voted monolithically for Democrats for 50 years with nothing to show for it. Baltimore, Washington DC, Chicago and every other city controlled by Democrats are hellholes of black misery, with black on black crime, out-of-wedlock births (fatherless households), high incarcerations, genocidal numbers of abortions and school dropouts. And yet, Democrats are still deceiving blacks with their tired old lie that every issue plaguing black Americans is the result of white racism.

My stomach turned upon hearing Democrat presidential candidate Elizabeth Warren promising that she will end environmental racism. I thought, "Here we go again with another Democrat attempting to fill blacks with more victim nonsense while trashing America, claiming that even the weather in the U.S. victimizes blacks!"

As the rabbi stated, viewing oneself as a victim does not empower you. It weakens you.

President Trump is the best thing for blacks since sliced bread. Under Trump, black unemployment is at an historic low. The record of Trump's extraordinary business career is filled with examples of advocating and hiring blacks. Branding Trump a racist is yet another evil Democrat lie to steer blacks away from a Republican who has implemented policies beneficial to them.

Unlike the Democratic Party, the Republican Party does not treat me like a poor inferior child in need of constant government intervention.

Folks, the bottom line is America is the greatest land of opportunity on the planet for all who choose to go for their dreams! This inspiring truth is as repulsive to Democrats as showing Dracula the cross.

Lloyd Marcus is a black Christian, conservative and Republican, renowned

as "The Unhyphenated American."
A prolific writer, Marcus' columns are
read worldwide. He has also appeared
on Fox News, CNN and Newsmax TV.
Marcus travels nationwide campaign-
ing with the Conservative Campaign
Committee to elect conservatives in
House and Senate races.

Highlights of Marcus' career include
performing for 1.7 million at the 2010
Rally to Stop Obamacare in Washington
DC. Marcus organized "Tea Are The
World," rallying musicians, singers and
bands to produce the "Taking Back
America/Tea Are The World" 44-song
CD album with proceeds benefiting
www.AmericasMightyWarriors.org.
The UK Guardian proclaimed Lloyd
Marcus the most prominent African-
American in the Tea Party Movement.

*Political commentator Armstrong
Williams explains why it is time
for blacks to "steal away" from
the Democratic Party.*

Steal Away to Freedom —
Escape the Democratic Party
Plantation, Sure: But to where?

Armstrong Williams

A news writer and commentator for
over thirty years, I have often written on
the subject of African Americans' blind
loyalty to the Democratic party. Unlike
any other major voting bloc, blacks tend
to vote overwhelmingly for Democrats.
So loyal have blacks been to the party
that they are taken completely for
granted by Democrats. As we approach
almost fifty years of black allegiance to
Democrats, the only thing Democrats
are offering blacks these days seems to

be a shelter from the fear of racism.
That is to say, every national election,
Democrats drum up fear of Republican
Party racism among blacks, driving
them to the polls, not because of what
they think they can gain by voting
for Democrats, but by fear of what
they potentially stand to lose by
having a Republican in office.

This rather Hobbesian choice begs
the question: If the Democratic party
is "Egypt" and blacks are enslaved
"Hebrews," where is the promised land
to which they are escaping? This is an
important question for two reasons.

Firstly, if you consider the way the
question is framed, it's all about stealing
away *from* the "Democrat Plantation."
Whereas the original negro spiritual
Steal Away has been interpreted as coded
reference for escaping slavery, the lyrics

actually say "steal away *to* Jesus." This
simple prepositional shift – *from* vs. *to* –
points to a vastly different orientation
on the part of our enslaved ancestors
as opposed to today's black voters.

Second, most of us complain about
our current situation. We hate our current
job and wish we could just quit; we are
no longer happy with our relationship
and wish we could just leave. We often
complain about these things, but rarely
envision the situation that we actually do
want. We all know what we don't want –
but what would an ideal job look like?
What would the features of an ideal
relationship be?

So, it is not enough to merely say
you'd like to escape the Democratic
plantation. Where would you like to
escape to? Would it be the Republican
Plantation? Seems to me that whatever

plantation you're on, you'd still be
a slave. Would it be to steal away to
freedom? If so, what does freedom
really look like? What options, risks,
responsibilities and rewards does
ideological freedom entail?

When we say that blacks need to steal
away from the Democratic Plantation,
we are not necessarily saying that
blacks should never vote for Democrats.
What we are saying is that blacks should
think broadly and strategically about
their interests – not merely based on
race – and consider which candidates
and political organizations are best
positioned to represent your interests
at a particular point in time. This would
be true political freedom. But it does
entail some risks and some perils.

There are no guarantees in life. But
to make the biggest gains often requires

deep insight into a particular situation,
and taking some risks. What are the risks,
for example, for blacks in supporting a
candidate like Donald Trump? Many
blacks think the risks are that Trump will
cut health care and other social services,
reduce civil rights protections for African
Americans, and foment a climate of
racism and division. But what are the
potential rewards of both voting for
Trump and having Trump in office?
The first would be having a seat at the
table. Without political participation,
it is hard to get a seat at the table where
you can hopefully influence policy in
some ways beneficial to your interests.
This seems especially true in the Trump
administration, which does not seem to
have as much of a settled agenda as most
previous administrations – but seems to
be an open contest of ideas and interests

among a revolving door of senior administration officials. It seems to be a place perfectly suited for political entrepreneurship and getting deals done from within.

Look for, example, how the deal on the *First Step Act* came together. Members of Trump's inner circle including Jared Kushner worked with moderate Republicans and Democrats in Congress, as well as key media allies including former Obama administration official Van Jones, and celebrities Kim Kardashian and Kanye West to create the first major criminal justice reform legislation in twenty years. And all this was done – from drafting to congressional passage to the President's signing it into law – in less than six months. Keep in mind, criminal justice reform was not a central plank of

Trump's original platform. But those
who had gained
a seat at the table and the President's ear
were able to shepherd the legislation
through Congress, and against the wishes
of the Republican leadership in Congress
and the Senate, very quickly.

Of course, not all policy initiatives
can be so easily crafted. For example,
education reform and health care reform
have proven to be somewhat intractable
issues in the current administration.
And here's how that can potentially work
to the benefit of black voters who are
thinking and voting strategically. Perhaps
the current stalemate over Obamacare is
a good thing. While Obamacare is
currently in place, blacks could focus on
the other side of the equation: that is,
jobs and entrepreneurship.

Again, there seems to be a major

impetus in the Trump administration towards fostering policies that will drive jobs and increase entrepreneurship. We currently sit at full employment, and African American employment is at a fifty-year high. Most of the new hires entering the work force in 2019-2020 are minority women. This is a deal we can live with in lieu of an enhanced social safety net. After all, freedom requires independent sources of income, and not dependence on government largesse.

For much of American history, since blacks gained the right to vote and began voting in larger numbers (beginning in the 1940s), blacks have traditionally formed a swing vote that could decide the outcome between equally divided white voting blocs. As such, politicians from both parties routinely courted the black vote – offering incremental gains in terms of civil rights as well as economic incentives. However, blacks are no longer putting themselves in a position to have strategic political leverage. By herding themselves into the Democratic party, the black vote is increasingly taken for granted, and is therefore less effective. Furthermore, there are opportunities out there among the other parties and candidates, that, if approached shrewdly and strategically, could help blacks achieve major progress towards what they do want: which is abundant life, greater liberty, and unfettered access to the American dream.

Armstrong Williams is the owner/ manager of Howard Stirk Holdings, and a well-known Political Commentator, Entrepreneur, Author, and Talk Show Host.

*Political commentator Kevin L. Martin
looks back on the destruction wreaked in
the black community by the Democratic
Party over the past 56 years.*

The Destruction of the Black Family Unit, the Fake Crimes Bill and the Emptiness of the Obama Era

Kevin Martin

I maintain that the Democrat Party has been able to do in 56 years what Slavery/Jim Crow/Segregation couldn't do in 400 years! Democrats have been able to destroy the Black Family Unit through the Government Mandated Social Reengineering which began in the late 1960s.

From Slavery through the Human (Civil) Rights Movement, the Black Family Unit led by Black Men has always been the driving force behind the

93

fight for our most basic "Human Rights."
Black men, women and children battled
slavery, Jim Crow and segregation with
nothing more than the power of our
bodies, defiance, determination and faith.

This power help changed the political
landscape in the early 1960s with the
election of President John F. Kennedy.
Blacks saw in Kennedy a politician
who was willing to pay more than just
lip service to helping blacks achieve
equality, but this was cut short with
President Kennedy's horrifying
assassination, which was a major blow
to the nation.

After becoming President, Lyndon B.
Johnson sought to keep the nation united
in fulfilling Kennedy's legacy, but when
it came to the issue of Human Rights for
Black Americans, he took a slower, more
cautious approach than Former President

Kennedy.

President Johnson, who had
previously been a U.S. senator from
Texas, was allied with several Southern
Dixiecrat Congressional Members,
who controlled powerful committees
in the Congress. President Johnson
knew he would need their approval for
appointments to the Federal Bench and
funding for our growing involvement
in Southeastern Asia.

President Johnson was willing to
comprise with these racist forces by
ensuring them that the federal
government, through renewable
legislation such as Civil, Housing
and Voting Acts, would only
acknowledge the most basic Rights
of Black Americans with a few
federal protections here and there

In my opinion, Democrats could never allow Black Americans to achieve this level of power as so, in order to prevent this from ever happening again, the Black Family had to be Socially Reengineered.

Many of those social programs promoted by Democrats as part of President Johnson's "Great Society" became the vehicle by which the Black Family Unit was reengineered. Blacks who migrated to the North and West for a better life were encouraged to apply for federal aid such as Section 8 Housing, food stamps, and reduced cost and free public-school lunch programs in their early years.

One of the requirements to qualify for these programs was that the income of any working-age male staying with his family would count against any aid received. I believe that this form of government-sanctioned family separation led to the raise of "generational welfare" in our poorer communities as the government took the place of black fathers. Black Men, who wanted to provide for their families and break the shackles of government dependence, often found it difficult to find worthwhile employment, being relegated low paying hourly jobs, while at the same time being shut out of unions and salaried position. Black Men found that they simply couldn't compete with government and, in the end, most lost their families to the system.

Single parent children found themselves caught up in a never-ending cycle of hopelessness and despair. This led them to simply give up. With substandard education, they lost their

self-esteem and pride. This, in turn,
lead them to turn to drinking and drugs.
Democrats exploited this situation for
political gain.

While drugs and alcoholism were
nothing new in poor black communities,
a new high exploded on the urban streets
in the mid-1980s in the form "crack
cocaine." Thus began what I called, "The
Crack Wars," lasting from 1986-1996.
Many of our poorer communities became
battlegrounds between rival gangs and
small-time hoods looking to cash in on
a quick buck. 300-500 murders a year in
major cities was not uncommon as local.
The Black community sought to unite
against this scourge as pressure was
applied on every level. Community
and academic activists worked with
levelheaded politicians and started to
come up with alternatives to this

epidemic, focusing on education and mentorships, that were effective.

Federal crime statistics peaked in 1991 and began to fall each following year. However, yet once again, Democrats under President Bill (or "Ole Triple K," as I call him) Clinton sought to use the Black community for their political gain in 1994 and stave off Congressional losses by Democrats by signing into law a totally unnecessary crime bill directly targeted at our communities based on the debunked myth that Urban Black Males were all "Super Predators," meaning that it would take decades, if ever to reform our Generational Criminal Mindset and prison was the best kind of treatment!

This racist narrative brought Bill Clinton a second term on the backs of thousands of black, who committed simple non-violent crimes along with actual violent criminals from our community.

By the early 2000s, Democrats realized that the empty promises, the scare tactics and self-appointed black leaders were wearing thin with the post-Civil Rights Era blacks, who were becoming the majority voting bloc in our community. Democrats needed a new vessel to shore up their most loyal voting bloc.

That vessel was Barrack Obama. White Democrats made sure to vet him properly in 2004 to ensure he had no connections to the Civil Rights Movement and could be used to pass the most socialist agenda since Johnson! Democrats would quickly label any opposition to him or their agenda through him as "racist!" (Remember in 2007,

then Senator Joe Biden refereed to
Presidential Candidate Barrack
Obama by saying, "I mean, you got
the first mainstream African-American,
who is articulate and bright and clean
and a nice-looking guy." "I mean this
is a storybook man.")

I firmly believe that Biden's
statement was code to ensure white
Democrats that it was okay to vote for
Obama for President in 2008 as "we can
control him and pass our most desired
agenda through him." Despite Obama
being black, I can't point to one piece
of legislation or Executive Order that
directly improved overall conditions in
Black America. Instead of President,
The Black Community got photo-op's
with Black Entertainers, empty Executive
Rhetoric (such as My Brother's Keeper,
and demands for complete Black Loyalty

(remember Michelle Obama told Black Residents in Baltimore in 2012, we must vote Democrat, no matter who is on the ticket) even as The Congressional Black Caucus was completely ignored for more than 720 days. The lasting effects of the failed crime's bill (whose failure can be seen in the need for Black Lives Matter now) was record Black Unemployment Numbers.

While some are finally making their Blexit now, I did so more than 24 years ago and haven't looked back yet because I am a proud Black Man, who believes in my own human rights and can form my own opinions, and I refuse to be anyone's victim for their political gain. I had the chance to meet then-candidate Bill Clinton at Southern University in Baton Rouge Louisiana in fall of 1992. The difference between what he campaigned on and the reality of how he governed was indictive of a Shadow Racist, who was only interested in how he could gain political from Black Americans. When I would confront White Liberals with this reality, they would feel that they had the right to chastise me over the fact that all the political gains post Slavery/Jim Crow/Civil Rights were due to them! This mindset is prevalent among White Democrats even in 2019 as Black Democrats are often employed as their attack dogs to lob false charges of Racist and White Supremacy against anyone who disagrees with their Pro-Socialist Agenda. To say I didn't see this coming in 1994 would indeed be an understatement!

Kevin L. Martin is a political commentator and subject matter expert with over 20 years of experience. On average, Mr. Martin does over 100 television and radio appearances yearly. After a distinguished seven-year career in the U.S. Navy as a Jr. Non-Commissioned Officer, Mr. Martin (along with his family) opened a private sector business in Washington DC. Mr. Martin has served as an advisor to National Center for Public Policy Research's Project 21 Network for over more than a decade. He joined Breitbart.com as a guest contributor in 2008 at the behest of the late Andrew Breitbart. Mr. Martin has been heard on national syndicated talk radio shows such as Sean Hannity, Mark Levin and many others.

High school teacher, father and part-time writer Jerome Danner discusses why blacks should question their deeply-held loyalty to the Democrats.

The Democratic Party Should Not Be the Only Party for Black People

Jerome Danner

Any belief not supported with some kind of evidence matching reality is of no earthly good. With this in mind, any Black person who has pledged an allegiance to the Democratic Party should ask themselves: do I have actual evidence of this party being a benefit to me? If we are really being honest, too many Black persons (with minds soaked in the waters of collectivist ideology) would express some view that equates to the *party of the Left* being the *party of the Black man.*

It is a misguided view to believe that
one party could represent the totality of
one particular race of people. Although
some well-known leaders may be
elevated to the level of being a kind of
voice of the people ("their people," i.e.,
Black people), it does not necessarily
mean that it is true that all of these
people will completely agree with that
one voice.

For example, someone as beloved
and revered as Dr. Martin Luther King,
whom many historians have made to
be the face of the 1960s Civil Rights
Movement, had his own opponents. He
always had to debate against others over
the social ideology that would be the
most provoking when it came to the fight
for minorities' rights. Nonviolence was
not for everyone, and King's view of it
did not sit well with Black leaders, such

as Malcolm X and Stokely Carmichael
(aka, Kwame Ture). But irrational beliefs
can be a strange thing. So much so that
some view a fellow person's decision
to go against the norm and adhere to
conservatism (or proclaim that Black
people do not have to be Democrats as
a well-known hip-hop artist, Chance the
Rapper, once said[30] through social media)
as some sort of cardinal sin. Many Black
conservatives have (figuratively) been
branded with the scarlet letters, "UT"
(for "Uncle Tom"), on their forehead for
daring to break with the conventional
thought that Black equals Democrat.

However, there is a real danger to
what I will call "settled generational
thinking." It is the kind of thinking that

---

[30]https://www.cnn.com/2018/04/25/politics/chan
ce-the-rapper-kanye-west-donald-
trump/index.html

is passed down from one generation to the next generation as if it is some kind of objective truth. But objective truth be told: it has never been thoroughly checked for its level of fact.

Believing something void of the truth makes one ignorant. It does not matter if it comes from someone that you trust. Some unfortunate souls may even try to accept the words of some infamous public intellectual as the foundation for the construction of their own principles. Nevertheless, if any doctrine is not tested against reality, then it should never be adhered to as some sort of law.

Dr. Thomas Sowell has pointed out before that intellectuals have the ability to be ignorant as well by proclaiming:

> Of all ignorance, the ignorance of the educated is the most dangerous. Not only are

educated people likely to have

more influence, they are the

last people to suspect that they

don't know what they are

talking about when they go

outside their narrow fields.[31]

All people, but especially Black folks, should heed these wise words. Black folks should question such a deeply-held loyalty to the Democrats. No one is even saying that you should then become a Republican. (That being said, most Black republicans/conservatives are typically able to debate rationally about what they believe.)

So, ask yourself: Is my support of the Democratic Party rational? Can I show evidence of how this particular party's

---

[31]https://twitter.com/thomassowell/status/117545
5402038874112?lang=en

policies have been beneficial to me?
If answers come back that affirm the
negative, then the only rational thing
to do is to say goodbye to that party
and try something new. That is if you
desire to be rational. Remember, no
matter how emotional your arguments
are, emotions alone do not impact change
nor do they make your beliefs true.

Jerome Danner is a high school teacher and part-time writer. He is a member of Project 21, which is an initiative of the National Center for Public Policy Research, and host of the "Thinking It Through" podcast, which is available on iTunes. Danner has written opinion pieces for popular websites such as *Medium, The Federalist, The Stream* and *The Spectator USA*. Additionally, he operates his own *Thinking It Through* website to "encourage civil dialogue and give thoughts on religion, culture, society and politics." When he is not providing commentary to the political and social issues of the day, he is busy teaching and chasing his two children!

Emeritus Professor of Political
Philosophy in the Department of
Political Science and Emeritus
Dean at James Madison College,
William B. Allen discusses why blacks
should move to the Republican Party.

Justifiably Proud:
The Standing of Blacks
in the Republican Party

W.B. Allen

Barack Obama launched his meteoric
political rise in 2004 by plagiarizing a
message published in my 1991 essay,
"Black and White Together: A
Reconsideration."[32] Unfortunately, while
he embraced the winning rhetoric, he did

---

[32] Published in *Reassessing Civil Rights,* edited
by Ellen Frankel Paul, Fred D. Miller, Jr., and
Jeffrey Paul (Cambridge, MA: Blackwell
Publishers for the Social Philosophy and Policy
Center, Bowling Green State University, 1991

not embrace the argument. Otherwise, he would have transformed the political character of our nation, for the first thing that he would have done would have been to lead the Democrat Party away from its practice of maintaining political ghettoes for minorities.

This observation is important in the present discussion because it highlights the primary reason why American Blacks should turn to the Republican Party. There is no alternative for them to stand on their own two feet in American politics. To be sure, leaders in the Republican Party for several decades past have feebly tried to imitate the Democrats by pursuing "constituency groups" as a recruiting tool. That stupid endeavor, however, did not sink the Party for the simple reason that the Party was saved by the evident reality that the

Democrats held a monopoly in that market.

It would now be timely for American blacks and Republicans to embrace the ultimate reality — the only winning opportunity that remains — which is to engage black men and women not on the basis of what the "party" or the "country" has to offer them but, rather, on the basis of what they have to offer the country. It is time to displace the question, "What have you got to lose?" with the question, "What have you got to give?"

That is the question that acknow-ledges that American blacks stand in a crucial position to bring aid to a country very much in danger of losing its way in a sea of identity politics. Moreover, it engages American blacks as standing on their own feet. No man or woman can be asked to shoulder the burden of deciding

a country's future when that man or
woman is not thought to be capable
of standing on his or her own feet. To
address American blacks as competent
— indeed, potential saviors of the nation
— is to demonstrate for them that respect
which their own self-respect demands.
It was always a mistake when people
imagined of Booker T. Washington that
his response to the question, "What is
to be done for the Negro?," "Leave him
alone!", meant that he was a racial
separatist. He was, instead, an advocate
of self-sufficiency for he understood
that it was only people who were self-
sufficient who could command enough
respect to win authority in the society.

For American blacks to exit the
political ghettoes of the Democrat Party
is far less a statement of disillusionment
than it is an assertion of self-sufficiency.

I have recently pointed out, in relation
to the "1619 Project[33]," that it is a myth
that only black people descend from
former slaves. Virtually all human beings
everywhere are the descendants of
slaves, serfs, peasants, coolies, or what
have you. Yet, it is only contemporary,
free black people who are expected to
wear the symbols of their forebears'
chains. Those symbols will not be
removed by the opinions of the people
who impose the requirement for such
self-identification. They can only be
removed when they are thrown off by
the people upon whom they are imposed.

---

[33] The 1619 Project is a program organized by
The New York Times in 2019 with the goal of
re-examining the legacy of slavery in the United
States and timed for the 400th anniversary of the
arrival in America of the first enslaved people
from West Africa.
(https://en.wikipedia.org/wiki/The_1619_Projec
t)

A truly brilliant essay by a college
student, Coleman Hughes, recently
published in *Quillette* (September 28,
2019, "The Case for Black Optimism"[34])
illustrates, relative to current policy
disputes, just how far American blacks
damage their own self-respect when
their attention is deflected from their
impressive attainments by the rhetorical
invocation of the "racial gap" along
almost line of human accomplishment.
Accepting the false "apples to oranges"
comparisons across the spectrum of
educational, income, incarceration,
unwed childbirth and other dynamics
produces a negative characterization
of the state of Black America that is
completely out of step with, in some

---

[34] Accessed October, 8, 2019 from:
https://quillette.com/2019/09/28/the-case-for-black-optimism/

cases, the geometric improvements in
Blacks' social condition. What Hughes
accomplished was to demonstrate how
a people with a cause for pride and self-
respect can nevertheless be induced to
view themselves as helpless victims. In
doing this, he fulfilled my expectation
when, in 1998, I led the Educational
Testing Services to abandon the use
of "racial gap" characterizations in
reporting test scores and to employ
the term "achievement gap." I meant,
then, of course, to induce an abandon-
ment of racial comparisons altogether,
something that did not occur.

This particular failure is related to
the persistence of political ghettoes
maintained by the Democrat Party.
The trope of racial comparison is so
far engrained in important dimensions
of our social and political life that there

is virtually no realistic expectation that
they will ever be willingly abandoned
by those most addicted to them. Thus,
the only corrective must come from the
refusal of the victims of such tropes to
give credit to them. And there is no way
to begin doing that save by exiting the
present political and social structures that
depend upon making such comparisons.
For that reason, a turn, a massive turn,
to the Republican Party would easily
and obviously be a major step in
declaring independence from the
subjugation of racial comparisons.

Such a step would work, however,
only if there exists a Republican Party
that could welcome the participation
of American blacks as fellow citizens
because they have a contribution to
make to the welfare of the country.
Many years ago, I delivered an address

in which I channeled Booker T. Washington by making the observation that a special burden lay on the shoulders of American blacks. That burden was to become the country's saviors — and thus the saviors of free government in the modern world. That was a lot to ask of a despised minority. The reality, however, was — and I believe, remains — that the country lacks any credible resource apart from what that despised minority can bring to the table to accomplish its full redemption.

Because the Republican Party lacks any toe-hold in the political ghettoes, it is ideally situated to become the vehicle for a new politics that would abandon ghettoization as a tool of political organization. It is, in fact, the only opportunity that exists for the emergence of the new politics.

If American Blacks moved to the
Republican Party to a significant degree,
they would become party to a new
founding generation re-defining the
future of the United States. That is the
only option remaining, in my view.

As I said at the outset, Barack Obama
failed. Although exposed to an argument
that would have led him to embrace such
a project — had he understood it — he
spurned the argument. That is the reason
I am certain of his plagiarism in 2004,
for he revealed in a subsequent address
that he had, indeed, read the essay from
which he drew inspiration without understanding. In the subsequent address, he
attacked an argument explicitly made
in the same essay, attributing it (as is
his wont) to "some conservatives."
The specific argument that I, and I alone,
had been making and had made in that

very essay. The details of the argument are not germane in these precincts (though related to the general theme of self-sufficiency). What does matter, though, is to observe that it is now reasonable for us to inquire just how many opportunities shall arise to reform our practices in this country, before no opportunity at all remains?

What I describe as a burden resting on the shoulders of Black men and women is not primarily an onerous duty. It is far rather a call for them to distinguish themselves as being able to see beyond the immediate contexture of events, to take the long view, and to aim for the kinds of distinction that enable peoples to command the respect of others by reason of the dignity and excellence of their attainments. The reason to move to the Republican Party is to demonstrate that we are justifiably proud to be Americans.

William B. Allen is Emeritus Professor of Political Philosophy in the Department of Political Science and Emeritus Dean, James Madison College, at Michigan State University. He served previously on the United States Council for the Humanities and as Chairman and member of the United Stated Commission on Civil Rights. He has published extensively, including *Re-Thinking Uncle Tom: The Political Philosophy of H. B. Stowe* (Lexington Books) and *George Washington: America's First Progressive* (Peter Lang, Inc.)

A member of the Florida House of Representatives, Mike Hill explains why he chose the Republican Party.

Why am I a Conservative Republican?
Mike Hill

The Democratic Party is the party of slavery, Jim Crow, the Ku Klux Klan and Planned Parenthood. All of these atrocities are enough to convince me that Democrats do not value individual freedom and liberty in the way that I believe Americans should.

The Democratic Party, with the help of Hollywood and the upper tiers of the media, has succeeded in reframing its place in black history while undermining the most fundamental parts of the black community: faith and family. The Democrats have put much effort into hiding their history.

The Republican Party was formed
because the Kansas-Nebraska Act
outraged a large part of the American
people. The Act proposed the expansion
of slavery. It allowed people in the
territories of Kansas and Nebraska to
decide for themselves whether or not
to allow slavery within their borders.
The Act served to repeal the Missouri
Compromise of 1820 which prohibited
slavery north of latitude 36°30′. This
pushed the country towards Civil War.
Our union was preserved by Abraham
Lincoln — a Republican.

While young black men my age were
nursing grievances imagined for them by
the Democratic Party, I was bending over
the rubble of Mussolini's Italy, picking
up remnants of a once great empire, now
small enough for me to hold in my hand
like a pebble. In Italy, among people

who had memories of bread lines and
mothers not yet grandmothers who
recalled the time when they pinched
their own babies to make them cry
dutifully before aid workers in order
to beg more persuasively for milk,
I learned about people and nations.

Perhaps it was the Lord's will that
I should be the son and grandson of two
men who promised their blood to protect
freedom in a time when the characters
of so many other young men were
being formed under the effects of
massive propaganda.

When I first ran for office, my
inspiration was to serve the people of
my District in Tallahassee. Somehow,
a lot of hopes were put upon me, as a
Conservative Republican, to evangelize
other black people or advise befuddled
fellow conservatives as to why the

126

Democratic Party has continued to fully
and overwhelmingly possess the majority
of black voters. I cannot speak to an
incomprehensible mass effect or delve
into the intricacies of propaganda that
so effectively transcends generations
of thinking and forms a crowd mind
of nearly insurmountable magnitude.
I can only speak for myself and how
I came to think for myself.

Early in life, at the core of my being,
I had a sense of individual identity.
I never based my behavior on the
opinion of others. Much to the chagrin
of my own colleagues and well-
intentioned natural allies, I don't
change how I think or act based on
what someone else thinks about me.
Thinking through the reason behind my
inclinations and perspective, they must
be historically rooted in my family's

service in the United States military. My grandfather served during World War II in a unit known as the "Harlem Hellcats." His unit was awarded the *Croix de Guerre* by France. My father served 26 years in the Air Force, active duty, a career that included service during the Vietnam War. I served in the US Air Force for 10 years upon graduation from the US Air Force Academy in 1980. My son was a US Marine, infantry, rifleman from 2014-2018.

Living abroad on military bases gave me a unique opportunity to explore other countries and cultures. The United States of America is different. It is special. It is important and exceptional. Our form of government is a culmination of man's most noble aims and divine blessing. I lived in Italy for nearly five years as

a pre-teenager and a teenager. While
living in Italy as a youth, not far from
the first seed of democratic thought,
I was standing on the same ground
that was once a great Republic, then
an empire, then a graveyard held up by
nothing but tombstones. Surely Italy had
seen its share of great individuals in its
vast history and indisputable influence
on Western Civilization? What will
prevent America from being buried by
its own crises or bending under its own
weight as a super power? The United
States Constitution is the standard for
making a great nation. The citizen is
the basic unit of a great nation. We must
ground ourselves in the Judeo-Christian
moral foundation necessary for the
Constitution to work.

I swore to protect and defend the
Constitution when I began my career in

the Air Force. I renew my oath daily as
a Citizen and as Member of the Florida
House of Representatives. I have
ultimate trust in the United States
Constitution to correct faults in
government and society. In America
you can always rise to the full
capabilities that God has instilled in you.
This happens as an individual, with
a vision, working towards that vision on
an individual basis, not as a member
of a group with which association may
be dubious, where one's efforts may
be put to the ends to serve a mob,
rather than a personal calling.

The Republican Party has a record
of preserving the American people and
the nation. I am a Republican because
the Party was born out of the necessity
of protecting and preserving what I
hold dear.

That is why I am a Republican.

Mike Hill was born at Scott Air Force Base in Illinois, and attended the United States Air Force Academy, from which he graduated in 1980. Following graduation, he joined the United States Air Force, serving from 1980 to 1990. While serving, Hill received the Air Force Achievement Medal, the Air Force Commendation Medal, the Air Force Organizational Excellence Award, and was named the Armament Division Company Grade Officer of the Year in 1988. He moved to Florida in 1985 and attended the University of West Florida, graduating with an MBA in 1988. He then worked as an insurance agent for State Farm Insurance. Following the death of Republican state representative Clay Ford, who had represented the second district since 2007, on March 18, 2013, Hill ran in the special election to replace Ford and defeated Scott Miller, Ed Gray, Mark Taylor, Jack Nobles and David Radcliffe in the Republican primary with 42 percent of the vote. He was endorsed in his primary campaign by the Pensacola News Journal, which declared that his "military experience, passion for open government, and business experience" made him the best candidate. In the general election, he faced Jeremy Lau, the Democratic nominee and a labor union official. Hill defeated Lau comfortably, which enabled him to become the legislature's only African-American Republican member.

Steal Away!

*A Tea Party organizer and a former
law enforcement officer, Emery W.
McClendon explains "how one
Black American sought truth and
was able to 'steal away' and
escape the Democratic stronghold."*

Wake Up, Walk Away,
and Don't Look Back!

Emery W. McClendon

In these time of uncertainty and
confusion in the Black community,
it's time for us to take a serious
look at where we want our lives and
communities to go. Blacks have
been lied to and mislead for too
long by the Democratic Party.

It is time for our leaders and the
people of our communities to seek
the truth.

Therefore I offer my life
experience as an example of how
one Black American sought truth
and was able to "steal away" and
escape the Democratic stronghold.

* * * * * ** * * * * ** * * * * *

When I was growing up, I was told
by everyone around me that I was to be
a proud Democrat; after all, they were
the party that cared for Blacks. I was
coached from birth that the Democratic
Party was the only party that provided
for and did anything for Blacks, so in
return I should be loyal to them.

We were taught that Republicans
were evil, mean and racist.

Day after day, week after week,
month after month, and year after year,
family and friends pounded this into
my head. I even heard it continually

at church.

I was even told that, when I became
eligible to vote, I had better vote
Democratic or not come home,
because I lived in a Democratic house.
My mother even worked for the Party.

Every four years my mother sat us
down in front of the TV to watch the
Democratic Party Convention. All of it!
We were indoctrinated and taught that
it was the party of choice.

We were not allowed to ask questions
or refute anything about the Party or its
platform — even though we were never
told what that platform was!

Most of the adults in my community really had no idea either; they
just followed the party because they
were told to do so by community
leaders, family, and friends. To stray
off of "the plantation" put you at risk

of exclusion in the community.

I had questions and I needed answers. My quest led me to begin to speak up at an early age. I questioned why Blacks were so loyal to a party that violated everything that we were taught as moral and Christian values. Most Blacks are very conservative.

It just didn't make sense to me. It was confusing to say the least.

My mother taught us conservative values along with sound Biblical Doctrine. However, what she taught us was in direct opposition to the principles of the Democratic Party platform. I'm not even sure if she realized that. She held to a Party first principle.

As a child I was taken to church almost every day of the week, and it wasn't an hour-long service either! They had church till the cows came home.

136

When I questioned the preachers about why they were Democrats, they always told me that they should never give people too much knowledge, because if they did the people wouldn't need them any longer. They said that it was necessary to keep people in darkness so that they would always be respected and be able to maintain a position as a community leader.

We would sit in church for hours upon hours as we heard the Word of God delivered to us with a mixture of politics in a very biased way.

It didn't make since to me, because it was like trying to drive a square peg into a round hole.

As you can imagine I got into a whole lot of trouble questioning authority, at home and abroad.

To make a long story short, I ended

up with a pretty sore behind, and a lot of hurt feelings, as well spending a lot of time in isolation.

I learned the meaning of the phrase "a hard head makes for a soft behind."

I was a target of verbal and physical discipline at home, at church, and in the neighborhood. I was called a heretic, a traitor, and was told to keep quiet. Many of the church leaders told me that I had the "Letter of the Law" but "no Spirit."

I eventually had to leave home, and my congregation, to search for the truth.

I enlisted in the military, but things were not any better there because the Blacks that I encountered were of the same mindset, and were also blind followers of the Democratic Party.

I sat down for hours with many of them discussing why they thought that I should be a good Democrat and kept

quiet. They never listened to my point
of view because they told me that it
was coming from a "white man's"
perspective, and that I was "not
black enough."

I was labeled an Uncle Tom, Mr.
Goody Two-Shoes, and a white man
in a black body; and I was targeted for
ridicule. I was even told that they were
going to kill me if I did not conform and
remember where it was that I came from.

After four years, I returned home.
Things hadn't changed. Friends and
relatives were still Democratic zombies.
They continued to harass me. I continued
to be a thorn in the side of the church
leaders and became the target of over-
the-pulpit rebuke, with no opportunity
to refute them.

I spent a lot of time in my early life
trying to reconcile this affection for their

blind allegiance to the Democratic Party.
I have never gotten any satisfactory
answers, just ridicule, and rebuke.

I finally decided to walk away from
it all and become a free thinker. It was
the best thing that I have ever done in
my life. A heavy load was lifted away.

I thank an older fellow co-worker for
helping me see the light, and pointing me
in the right direction.

I have since learned about Freedom,
Liberty, and the true meaning of the
American Dream. I have become
engaged in efforts to help others leave
the Democratic Plantation by informing
them of the truth, truth that can easily
be found if you are willing to search for
it and change.

It hasn't been easy.

I've spread conservative principles
and the truth about the American Dream

ever since. Some listen, but many refuse to hear the message because the truth doesn't matter to them. Most of those that do agree will not openly declare it for fear of retribution. They want to be accepted in the community.

It's been a tough fight, and an uphill journey, but I'll never turn back. The truth will make you free.

Even after suffering the loss of family and friends I will continue to choose conservative ideas over progressive lies because they lead to independence and prosperity.

Much of what happens to us Blacks regarding the implanting of our worldview takes place early on in life. It's implanted deep in our hearts, and it's tough to root it out. It takes place in the home, at church, and in the community. Most of it is forced upon us by peer pressure.

It is a result of tribalism and identity politics.

Sadly, much of what is taught is based on bad history, bias, and hate, not on facts.

For most of our lives Blacks are taught to be loyal to each other, even with our vote. Unity is based on skin color, not on truth, whether it is Biblical or political. What a travesty.

It's past time to make a change.

Many are coming around, and hearts are changing, but we have a long ways to go. Ignorance and poor leadership are destroying blacks.

Our nation's future is at stake.

Thank God for the many Black conservatives that are spreading the truth; it's a breath of fresh air for our communities.

Thank God I became a thinker
way back in the eighties! Will you
"walk away" and do the same today?

Emery W. McClendon is a Tea Party
Organizer and a member of Project 21.
He served in the U.S. Air Force and the
Indiana Air Guard. He is a former Ft.
Wayne Police Reserve Officer, Allen
County Sheriff Deputy, and Indiana
State Trooper. He is a contributor to:
Politichicks, The Federalist, and
The Veterans Voice.

A published writer who is currently studying at Emory University Law School, Stone Allen Washington explains that he never had to leave the Democrat Party because he was fortunate enough to be born outside of the plantation, raised by a Black conservative father.

The Apotheosis of Black Conservatism and the Escape from the Democrat Party Plantation

Stone Allen Washington

I am a black, dyed in the wool
Republican, and I never intend
to belong to any other party
than the party of freedom.

Frederick Douglass

Unlike so many Black conservatives
today, I never had to leave the Democrat

144

Party in the first place. I was fortunate enough to be born outside of the plantation, raised by a Black conservative father. This is based on the wise proverb by the Abolitionist icon, Frederick Douglass, who stated, "It easier to build strong children than to repair broken men." My father, Professor Ellis Washington, spent his early years temporarily imprisoned in what he himself called a "de facto Democrat" until he came to leave the party after a series of epiphanies during his senior year at DePauw University, reaching its crescendo on Christmas Day, 1983. This political awakening grew during President Ronald Reagan's second term in office, and this apotheosis and devotion to conservatism would help him have the foresight to be one of the few to agree with the legendary GOP

maker, Lee Atwater, that George H.W.
Bush must nominate Donald J. Trump
as his Vice President at the 1988 GOP
Convention in New Orleans. Much to
my father's dismay, Bush would instead
choose a political simpleton, Sen. Dan
Quayle (R-IN), who ironically enough
also attended DePauw.

The apotheosis of Professor Ellis
Washington occurred in the context of
writing his first published essays—*Birth
of a Conservative Intellectual, Part I
and Part II*. Here is a short narrative
from Part II of that apotheosis to
embrace a conservative worldview:

> What provoked me to write
> these essays was my vexation
> at the low level of intellectual
> rigor of our school newspaper.
> I grew weary of knowing what
> the sororities and fraternities

did at their parties, who won
the football, basketball and
baseball games, or what girl
would become homecoming
queen. I wanted to read
something substantive,
something intellectually
compelling, something that
could improve the character,
enlighten the mind, yea ...
even help fulfill the destiny
of the reader! As I mused on
this and the paradigm shift
I was compelled to make
during Christmas break
1982, I thought: why not
write something myself?

Since leaving the restraints of the
Democrat Socialist Party, Professor
Washington has never once looked
back. For as long as I've been alive,

my father has raised me to be a free and
independent critical thinker, training me
to better understand the advantages and
benefits of championing conservative
principles, yet never neglecting the
serious study of other ideas so as
not to become myopic or parochial
in one's thinking.

As a conservative black college
student, I've had my fair share of
arguments, accusations and insults.
But I refuse to back down. Here's why.

I've learned from my father, Professor
Ellis Washington, that we are free to
choose our own path; one that can and
should diverge from the Democrat Party
— the perceived norm for Black people.

My father taught me how the Left
has a dark history of despising
the combination of "Black" and
"conservative," which shatters their

148

warped paradigm of how all Blacks owe allegiance to the Democrat Party, envisioning themselves as the party that freed Blacks from slavery and condemned racism (they didn't, it was the Republicans).

In a sense, I have freed my mind from the invisible chains of servitude to a party I owe nothing to, yet a party that demands my allegiance.

As a history major, I've learned how Black people originally voted predominately for the Republican Party, since being granted freedom from slavery, provided citizenship and the right to vote by President Abraham Lincoln.

In reality, Blacks ultimately owe their freedoms to the Republican and abolitionist forces that fought for their equal rights against those who battled for

their enslavement, the Democrat
plantation owners and Confederates.

And when I look around today,
I don't see the Democrat Party doing
any favors for the Black community.
Their policies have kept us on welfare,
positioning us as helpless victims
who must rely on the government
for salvation... No thanks!

Despite my race voting 94 to 97
percent Democrat in most political races,
I will not allow skin color to dictate my
own political beliefs.

I first came to appreciate conservative
ideals during my sophomore year at
Grosse Pointe South High School, where
I joined my school's Young Americans
for Freedom (YAF) chapter in April
2013. The same week that I joined YAF,
our group would host former Senator
Rick Santorum (R-PA) to speak at the

school, representing the most prominent
speaker ever to visit since my school
hosted Dr. Martin Luther King exactly
45 years earlier (April 4, 1968). I
commemorated this historic event shortly
after Santorum's speech, in addition to a
50th year commemoration in 2018, in a
column entitled, "1968-2018: Honoring
the 50-year Legacy of Martin Luther
King and the 'Other America.'"
(https://www.renewamerica.com/
columns/swashington/180419)

The Sen. Santorum event was nearly
cancelled over a dispute regarding his
conservative philosophy (even in a
supposedly "conservative" city like
Grosse Pointe, Michigan), creating a
vortex of controversy in the days prior.
Then Superintendent of Grosse Pointe
schools, Tom Harwood (who was later
fired over a series of unfortunate events),

complained about Santorum's defense of traditional marriage as offending his gay brother. As a result of this misguided complaint, students had to convince their parents to sign permission slips to attend the event, which only inspired more people to attend, packing our large gym to the rafters!

I assisted in preparations for the event; helping to seat the students and teachers in the fully packed gym. Santorum gave a rousing and inspirational speech that would remain ingrained in the minds of the hundreds of students who attended, many of them previously unexposed to a viewpoint contrary to the progressive politics preached in modern public education. This historic event would mark one of my first introductions into conservative activism.

Steal Away!

In the month of March preceding Santorum's visit, I delivered my first ever public speech at the Metropolitan Detroit Freedom Coalition (MEDEFCO). The speech would be the first of a series of addresses I would give to honor Dr. Martin Luther King and the 45th anniversary of him delivering his famous "Other America" speech at my high school on March 14, 1968. The speech symbolized my father's and my unyielding appreciation of Dr. King's prophetic speech, delivered in an all-white suburb of Detroit during the pinnacle of the Civil Rights movement, just three weeks before his assassination.

After high school, I would become more and more inspired by conservative ideals and Natural Law/Natural Rights principles imparted to me by my father due to his expertise in law and politics.

153

I learned from my father's experiences as a black conservative intellectual, teaching me crucial critical thinking skills pertaining to political discourse. My unique position as a black conservative writer has allowed me to voice my political beliefs on a number of academic disciplines and expound on how they compare with the toxic environments in Liberal-dominated colleges.

In a special op-ed piece for *The College Fix* (https://www.thecollegefix. com/im-black-and-conservative-the-democrats-dont-own-me/), I wrote later in September 2013, I reveal my conservative beliefs and status as one of the few black conservatives at my alma mater of Clemson University. Later during my freshman year of college in Sept. 2015, I attended George Mason

University where my father made sure
that I met weekly with his mentor of 30+
years – the venerable black conservative
economics scholar, Dr. Walter Williams.

After I transferred to Clemson for my
sophomore to senior years, I found
myself in a unique position in
comparison to my fellow Generation
Z'ers and Millennials, who were either
politically apathetic or embraced more
socialist ideals than I. For example,
during my sophomore year at Clemson,
in the midst of the final weeks leading
up to the 2016 Presidential election,
I recall in many of my classes
vociferously debating with the majority
of my fellow classmates about who
would win the election. Like the walls
of Jericho separating the Israelites from
the Canaanites, I was separated from the
rest by being the only one in my political

science classes who openly believed
Donald Trump would win the
presidency. This divergence was greatest
in my Political Elections class, where
I argued with nearly 50 other students.
Most of them unquestionably believed
that Hillary Clinton would easily defeat
Donald Trump and anyone who dared to
predict otherwise was considered crazy
and openly laughed at and mocked.
I speak on this perilous odyssey that
I would face alone in my *College Fix*
op-ed:

> Despite even my conservative
> professor and mentor, Dr.
> David Woodard, not voting
> for President Trump, I
> wholeheartedly declared
> Trump would carry a landslide
> victory in the election and
> firmly argued my case against

conservative and liberal
students alike. And on the
week following Election Day,
my professor even surprised
the class by buying a chocolate
cake, in honor of Trump's
unexpected victory and my
firm belief in him winning.

After Trump's victory on Election
Day Nov. 8, 2016, that cake not only
gave me sweet taste of victory, but it was
even more symbolic when Dr. Woodard
made the most pro-Hillary Clinton
student (and my friendly nemesis), Maria
Petromichelis, cut my slice of the cake in
front of the whole class. While the pain
of her candidate losing was apparent, she
and others would later fondly reminisce
about our heated debates in class.

In addition to Dr. Woodard's class,
I recall debating his dear friend, Dr.

Bruce Ransom, who was also a
mentoring figure for me. Dr. Ransom
would often take the side of his 12 other
students in my Urban Politics class, all
of whom believed without a doubt that
President Trump would lose the election.
Despite us being at odds politically, Dr.
Ransom would grow fonder of having
me as his student protégé at Clemson
alongside Dr. Woodard. As Clemson's
resident free-thinking black conservative,
I would always defy the status quo and
make things more exciting for both of
their classes.

Professors Woodard and Ransom
consistently guided me throughout my
time at Clemson, providing invaluable
wisdom, political advice and even
recommendation letters. One such
recommendation helped pave the path
for my acceptance into the highly

competitive Young Leader's Program at The Heritage Foundation. At Dr. Woodard's guidance, I took the spring semester of my junior year off to intern at The Heritage Foundation in the Legacy Society. Working in the development department, I assisted a special group of donors who intended to make The Heritage Foundation part of their wills, trusts, and estate plans. Similar to my predicament at Clemson, I was a minority figure at The Heritage Foundation, being one of only two Black students in the incoming intern class of 60. Yet surprisingly, my class would witness the first time in the organization's 45-year history that a black woman, Kay Coles James, would become President of the Foundation. Alongside my intern class, Mrs. James began work on January 8th, 2018.

I would often see Mrs. James, for her
office was located just down the hall
from where I worked in the Development Department.

My greatest memory at Heritage
came when the intern class was afforded
the opportunity to personally hear from
the Honorable Justice Clarence Thomas.
(He was my father's first legal mentor
31 years ago, when he was a law student
alongside Barack Obama at Harvard,
and due to my father's recommendation,
Justice Thomas has been my intellectual
mentor since 2016.) On that day, my
intern class was invited to an exclusive
three-hour Q&A session with Justice
Thomas in East Conference Room of
the illustrious Supreme Court building.
There, a formal picture of our entire
intern class surrounding Justice
Thomas was taken by a professional

160

photographer. Afterwards, our group crossed into an adjacent room where we were seated and given the opportunity to hear from Justice Thomas up-close and personal. Following a brief speech, Justice Thomas opened the floor to questions for the remaining two hours that we had with him. My group asked many compelling questions surrounding Justice Thomas's long-time role on the Court, including his position on the Second Amendment, and traits that make for an ideal candidate to clerk for him. Excitingly, I was soon given the opportunity to ask a question, deciding to first make known to my fellow interns that this wasn't the first time Justice Thomas and I had met.

I reminded Justice Thomas that we first personally met in December 2016 when I had lunch with him and his good

friend Dr. Walter Williams, the John M.
Olin Distinguished Professor of Economics at George Mason University.

Remembering our meeting, Justice
Thomas asked how my father, Professor
Ellis Washington, was doing, to which
I happily responded that he was doing
very well. Justice Thomas has been an
intellectual mentor to my father for the
past 31 years, as Professor Washington
has dedicated many of his 30+ law
review articles, hundreds of scholarly
articles and more than half of his 11
books specifically to Justice Thomas.
For example, the five volumes of my
father's ground-breaking book series,
*The Progressive Revolution: History
of Liberal Fascism Through The Ages*,
have had the unique honor of all being
accepted into the Chamber's Library
of the Supreme Court.

162

Steal Away!

My question posed to Justice
Thomas was this: "What advice would
you provide to newly appointed
Associate Justice, Neil Gorsuch, to honor
the late Justice Antonin Scalia, upon
replacing him on the Court?" Justice
Thomas replied that it was not his place
to direct Justice Gorsuch's steps, or for
him to fill anyone's shoes. He believed
that Justice Gorsuch would chart his
own uniquely special path forward,
and only hoped that Gorsuch would do
the Framers proud in abiding by the
Constitution with a faithfully Textualist
and Strict-Constructionist interpretation,
as he himself has devotedly done since
his nomination was affirmed by the
Senate on October 15, 1991.

In conclusion, I am honored to
declare myself an independent-minded
black conservative, unrestrained by

the dystopia of the Democrat Party Plantation Groupthink or wearing the shackles of socialist slavery. In today's America, there is evidence that a growing number of Blacks are abandoning the Democrat Party. An example of this can be seen in recent polls indicating that blacks are thrilled by President Trump's booming economy and creation of 6.5 million new jobs. As of September 2019, black unemployment and the black-white employment gap have fallen to the lowest levels ever recorded. More and more Blacks are becoming "woke" and having second thoughts about being used and abused under failed Democrat Party policies. Recent poll numbers show that Trump's approval ratings are up among minorities, with popularity to Black American voters rising to 25%, along with support among Hispanic voters at 50%.

Steal Away!

These and so many other
factors contribute to a growing shift,
a national wave of optimism among
disenfranchised blacks seeking
relief from the misery of invidious
discrimination under Democrat
leadership, which amounts to only
welfare dependency, inner-city poverty,
crumbling school systems, disarming
innocent gun owners, and many more
grotesqueries. This is why I thank
God every day to have been born an
independent conservative, hoping that
one day my minority position will turn
into a majority status, as more and more
blacks abandon the Democrat Plantation,
abiding by the iconic words of that
great Abolitionist Frederick Douglass:

I prayed for freedom for twenty
years, but received no answer
until I prayed with my legs.
                        Frederick Douglass

165

References

- Stone Washington, *Dreams from my father: A story of a blacklisted conservative black scholar,* (July 31ˢᵗ, 2018).
- Stone Washington, *I'm black and conservative. The Democrats don't own me,* (June 6ᵗʰ 2018).
- Stone Washington speaks at the Metropolitan Detroit Freedom Coalition (MEDEFCO), March 2013.
- Ellis Washington, Trump with Lee Atwater (GOP Convention, New Orleans, LA 1988) @ http://www.elliswashingtonreport.com/2 018/09/22/birthday-essay-manchild-lebron-james-vs-heman-president-trump-guess-who-wins-america/.
- Stone Washington, Justice Clarence Thomas, Generation Z, and Me, April 4ᵗʰ, 2016.
- Ellis Washington, *The Progressive Revolution: Liberal Fascism Through The Ages (vols. I-V).*
- Project 21 Press Release, *Record-Low Black Unemployment Cheered by Black Activists- Project 21 Members Credit Trump Economic Policies for Increased Minority Opportunity*, September 9ᵗʰ 2019.

166

- Joanne Marie Hoopes and Roger Weber, *Rick Santorum visits Grosse Pointe South High School to give speech on leadership*, April 24th, 2013.
- Young American's Foundation, *Grosse Pointe South High School Reverses Santorum Decision.*
- Stone Washington, *1968-2018: Honoring the 50-year legacy of Martin Luther King and the other America*, April 19th, 2018.
- David Catron, *Why Trump's Approval Ratings Are Up Among Minorities*, August 19, 2019.
- Ellis Washington, *Birth of a Conservative Intellectual, Part I*, February 1st, 2013.
- Ellis Washington, *Birth of a Conservative Intellectual, Part II*, February 9th, 2013.
- Philip Bump, *Mostly black neighborhoods voted more Republican in 2016 than in 2012*, September 25th, 2017.

Stone Washington is currently
studying in the Juris Master Program
at Emory University Law School. He is
a recent graduate of Clemson University
with a bachelor's degree in history and
a minor in political science.

Stone was a summer 2019
journalism fellow at *The Daily Caller*,
sponsored by The College Fix. In 2018,
he participated in the Young Leader's
Program at the Heritage Foundation,
where he interned in the development
department. He is also a five-year
alumnus of Envision youth leadership
conferences.

He is a published writer, with work
appearing on Professor Ellis Washington's website – *Ellis Washington Report*.
Stone has also been published by *Renew
America*, *College Fix*, *Campus Reform*
and *Red Alert Politics*.

*Recipient of a master's degree and
a doctoral degree in economics at
George Mason University and founder,
director, and chief developer of the
website BlackEconomics.org, Brooks B.
Robinson asks an important question.*

Why Not a Black Political Party?

by

Dr. Brooks B. Robinson

August 15, 2015

©BlackEconomics.org

Overview

For Black Americans, which critical
questions surface when considering
political parties? As the 2016 presidential
election approaches, the duopolistic
political parties (the Republican and
Democratic parties) promise to continue
their domination of the political
landscape. While the status quo is often

considered to be efficient, one must
wonder why a two-party system
dominates and why there are not more
political parties in the US. At bottom,
what do political parties do? Moreover,
a very important question that warrants
a forthright answer is, why is there no
Black political party? Despite our social
fragmentation, we should ask: Given a
40-plus million population with well over
20 million eligible voters, why have we
Black Americans not organized ourselves
into a political party that can leverage
this sizeable voting bloc to obtain
political, economic, and social benefits?
In addition, given that we generally vote
as a bloc and serve as a median vote,[35]
does not forming a Black political party

---

[35] See section on "Important and simple realities"
below.

appear to be a very logical strategy?
This essay explores answers to all of
these questions, proposes a strategy
for establishing a Black political party,
and suggests that the time for moving
forward on this strategy is now.

Introduction

This essay is about political parties.
We begin with several important
questions about political parties, the most
important of which may be, "Why is
there no Black political party?" Beyond
the critical questions, we note two
important realities about Black votes.
We ask: "Why did earlier efforts to raise
a Black political party fail?" In the end,
it will take leadership to initiate efforts
to organize a Black political party.
Therefore, we inquire why notable and
relatively wealthy Black Americans
have not sought to solidify a legacy for

themselves by seeking to raise a Black political party. We end the essay by highlighting what a Black political party may actually be able to accomplish, and we issue a call for this effort to be undertaken in the near term.

From our perspective, the formation of a Black political party is a logical objective that is already in place on a *de facto* basis with little-to-no benefits for the average Black Americans. It seems the right thing to do to formalize a Black political party so that average Black Americans can at least effect positive efforts to gain benefits through a tried-and-true political process.

Questions that baffle the mind

When a Black American begins to think seriously about political parties in the US, s/he usually gets around to the following two questions:

1. Why aren't there more political parties in the US—a nation that prides itself on democracy, which is supposed to be all about voice?

2. What do political parties do?

The first question is very baffling because so many of the world's democracies operate with few-to-many political parties. The argument has long been that it is easier to get things done with just two parties as opposed to many. The recent history of gridlock in the American political system calls this argument into question.

As a possible explanation for a two-party system, we surmise that two is a good number for those who want to employ the old tricknology that has worked to bamboozle and hoodwink the world for the last 6,000 years. It is an effective divide-and-conquer scheme.

Moreover, when one accounts for the centrist stances that are often adopted in the end by political candidates, essentially, one ends up with a blending of the two political parties, i.e., one basic position on which the polity votes.

The second question is not so baffling, but it appears to be little understood. In the party of the US President and of the two houses of Congress, one has the forces that not only establish the nation's legislative agenda, but often, by default, its economic agenda as well. For Black Americans, who are at the bottom of the nation's economic ladder, it makes sense that we would be very interested in influencing the economic agenda and would, therefore, have a strong interest in influencing political outcomes through the political party process.

But there is a third question, which, given the foregoing, is most baffling:

3. Why isn't there a Black political party?

As already mentioned, it may very well be the goal of the most powerful in the country to restrict political parties to two to give the appearance of choice: between a wolf and a fox. In the end, as Malcolm X pointed out, they are both members of the dog family. They have shown historically that they have not had an inherent interest in the best outcomes for Black Americans. Every important legislative economic victory that Black American have won, and there have been only a few, have required considerable sacrifice on our part: Lives lost, physical injury, jail time, protest time, and a scar on our historical psyche. So, efforts have always been afoot to thwart attempts to

establish or maintain a "third" party—
especially a Black political party.

Nevertheless, given a Black
population of 40 plus million in 2015,
and with over 25 million 18 years or
older and eligible to vote, it seems
reasonable that we would want to
leverage this political power to obtain
good for ourselves.[36] The answer to
"why there is no Black political party"
will come forth as we proceed.

Important and Simple Realities

The first simple reality comes out of
research conducted by Black (1948).
He is credited with having identified
the underlying logic of the "median vote
theorem." It is an important theorem
because it characterizes a very favorable

---

[36] These statistics were derived from Colby and
Ortman (2015) and File (2015).

outcome for Black Americans. In essence, when all votes are organized along a linear political spectrum, the vote that is at the median (half on one side and half on the other) is the one that carries the day — wins the election. In the US, where the Democratic and Republic parties nearly split the total vote (including whites and other ethnic groups — excluding Blacks), the Black vote usually represents the median vote and, therefore, decides most major elections.[37]

Walton (1969) makes it abundantly clear that the two major parties and many third parties understood this situation very well. He points out that as early as

---

[37] Of course, Hispanics, another important ethnic group in the nation, can argue the same. When the total vote excluding Hispanics is split on a political issue, then Hispanics can claim a median vote position.

1843, the Liberty party appointed Negro
delegates to high positions on various
committees. The Free Soilers elected
Frederick Douglass as Secretary of their
1852 political party convention. The
Peoples' or Populists' party and the
Progressive party sought actively and
vigorously Black membership in the late
19th and early 20th century, respectively.
The doctrinal (Socialist and Communist)
parties found it important to their
development to seek to attract Black
membership. It goes without saying that
the Republican and Democratic parties
have mixed histories concerning their
interest in securing Black membership.
Nevertheless, when politically expedient,
all of these parties resorted to efforts to
attract the Black vote. Therefore, Black's
theorem was well understood long before
he espoused it, and it remains true today.

Given our advantageous position in the political strategic game, it makes sense that Black Americans would want to isolate ourselves to maintain our median voter position. One of the best ways to do this is to form our own political party, and to use that political party to leverage that median vote to secure the related benefits that can be secured.

The second simple reality is that Black Americans have essentially acted as our own political party historically. That is, Blacks have been nearly monolithic in our voting— either voting for the Republican Party, when it was the party of Lincoln, and later for the Democratic Party, as the party of Roosevelt, Kennedy, Johnson, Carter, Clinton, and Obama.

In other words, we vote mainly as
a bloc, which is consistent with voting by
political parties. For example, in 2012,
76% of Black Americans polled
indicated that they were Democrats; 5%
said they were Republicans; 16% were
Independent; and 3% were affiliated with
other political parties or did not know
their affiliations.[38] When we form our
own political party, voting as a bloc is
likely to continue. The important change
will be that we will have operationalized
an organizational structure that can
leverage more effectively the power of
our voting bloc.

Forming a Black political party and
voting as a bloc may seem anomalous
in light of the nearly 50-year trend of
the four-way disintegration of Black

---

[38] See Pew Research Center (2012).

America.[39] We believe that this trend is by design. However, we can design an effort to reverse the trend. Is it not logical that we look into the future and envision a path that is most favorable for us?

Political strength is in numbers. Therefore, we should see the future benefit of leveraging our growing population and median voter status and make a decision to form a Black political party that can produce the benefits that we desire.

Why earlier efforts to raise a long-standing Black political party failed

Beginning in earnest in the early 1960s, Black political parties in their two varieties (parallel/satellite and independent parties) sprang up to give

---

[39] See Robinson's (2010) analysis of the four primary Black American groups.

voice to Black Americans' fundamental rights and critical needs. Walton (1972) does a superb job of chronicling the rise and disappearance of these parties. They focused mainly on local and state politics: e.g., the Mississippi Freedom Democratic Party (MFDP); the Lowndes County Freedom Organization (LCFO, also known as the Black Panther Party); and the National Democratic Party of Alabama (NDPA).[40] Who can forget Fannie Lou Hamer's exploits at the 1964 Democratic National Convention in Atlantic City, New Jersey? However, probably the most instrumental personality in the rise of these political parties was Stokely Carmichael (aka

---

[40] The Black Panther Party mentioned here is different from the Black Panther Party for Self Defense that was founded in 1966 in Oakland, California by Huey P. Newton.

Kwame Ture) who, *inter alia*, coined the phrase "Black Power" as part of his efforts to build support for Black political parties in Mississippi.

Moving forward to the late 1960s and the early 1970s, Black political parties with strong national interests surfaced. The most notable of these parties were the Peace and Freedom Party and the National Black Political Convention, which led to the formation of the National Black Political Assembly. While the latter was well-organized and attracted significant support (at least initially), only the former actually placed Black candidates on presidential ballots.[41]

Walton (1972) reveals that a lack of political maturity on the part of

---

[41] The Peace and Freedom Party placed Eldridge Cleaver and Ronald Daniels on presidential ballots in 1968 and 1992, respectively.

the parties' members prevented each
of these Black political parties from
achieving significant longevity. In
combination, a failure to attract enough
Black votes, the absence of sufficient
financial support, internal conflicts and
defections, and changing times (mainly
integration of the American society
including political parties) caused
Black political parties to dissolve,
align with other third parties, or merge
with the two major political parties.

It could be argued that the latter
reason is the most important contributor
to the demise of Black political parties.
It is true that all of these Black political
parties had as a *raison d'être* opening
doors to Black political participation
in the nation. Once the nation began to
soften on permitting Black participation
in political affairs, the primary extant

reasons for the existence of Black
political parties faded.

But, as always, things change as
time elapses. In this case, Black
Americans now have new strategic
political, economic, and social interests
and, therefore, have new reasons for
forming a Black political party.
Therefore, the operative question is:
"How do we raise one?"

Want to leave a legacy?

The difficulties that were
experienced historically in raising and
sustaining a Black political party should
not discourage current-day leadership
that is interested in optimizing political
outcomes for Black Americans. In fact,
it seems reasonable that selected
relatively wealthy Black Americans
who have dabbled in politics as
important promoters of candidates

should have a desire to solidify their

legacies in this life by collaborating

to raise a Black political party today.

Think of Oprah Winfrey, Richard

Parsons, Kenneth Chenault, Russell

Simmons, Jay-Z, and Beyoncé. Add in

a few wealthy athletes such as LeBron

James, Michael Jordan, Magic Johnson,

and up-and-comers, such as Cam Newton

and Russell Wilson. Together, they

represent a solid base for gathering the

finances and the wherewithal to start a

process of raising a Black political party.

Add in Cathy Hughes (the founder of

the media company Radio One), and we

will have access to at least a couple of

television networks and a radio network

to use to publicize the effort. What

greater legacy would one want to leave

behind, which could (like the current

Democratic and Republic Parties) stand

for well over 150 years?

It is nearly impossible, today, to
evolve the type of legacy that has been
left to us by the likes of Paul Cuffee,
Gabriel Prosser, Denmark Vesey, David
Walker, Nathaniel Turner, Frederick
Douglass, Booker T. Washington,
W.E.B. DuBois, Marcus Garvey, Elijah
Muhammad, Rosa Parks, Malcolm X,
or Martin Luther King, Jr. However,
by making an effort to raise a Black
political party, the aforementioned
wealthy Black personalities of today
could defy the status quo and strike
a blow for securing equal rights and
benefits for Black Americans.

We should not expect that a Black
Political Party can or should emerge
in full bloom. We should recall that in
1854, today's Republican Party began
with a gathering of a few committed

activists in a one-room schoolhouse in Ripon, Wisconsin. Consider the party's power today. Similarly, a Black political party can grow, over time, into a powerful instrument, which can wrest from the political process in this country the types of benefits that we so richly deserve.

To achieve such growth, the Black American body *politique* cannot afford to sit and do nothing. If wealthy Black Americans light the political party fire, then every eligible Black American voter should keep the fire burning by being a card-carrying party member of the new party and should reflect political maturity by contributing financially and politically to the party on an ongoing basis.

What can a Black political party do?

In short, the answer to this question is: "The same things that the two major

political parties can do, but probably on
a smaller scale." After some thought,
one may arrive at four important
objectives that a Black political party
might achieve—at a minimum.

1. Create what Black America needs
   most: Operational jobs as well
   as jobs in the broader economy.
   In other words, a Black political
   party must have operational
   staff members across the nation.
   More importantly, assuming
   that the party is able to operate
   effectively, it should be able to
   influence social and economic
   policies in order to create
   continuously a significant supply
   of new jobs for Black Americans
   in the broader economy.

2. Linked to the first objective, a
   Black political party should be

able to create leverage for Black
Americans and enable us to obtain
more of the benefits that we desire
from the US political, economic,
and social systems. Critical to
this objective, a well-organized
party should enable us to punish
politically those who defect from
the political strategy that we
establish for ourselves.

3. Linked to the second objective,
   a Black political party should help
   us to assemble a structure that
   can facilitate the formulation
   and monitoring of a long-term,
   political, economic, and social
   strategic plan—something that has
   been sorely missing from our play
   in the national strategic game from
   the outset.

4. As an excellent side-benefit,
   a Black political party should
   enable us to extend our knowledge concerning how to operate
   political systems in the event
   that we found a nation of our
   own at some point in the future.

If a Black political party satisfies all
or most of these objectives, then it would
have been well worth its creation. As
already discussed, we have a history of
creating political parties, and even
managing major political parties in the
US. For example, Ron Brown served as
Chairman of the Democratic National
Committee in the late 1980s and early
1990s and was instrumental in securing
the presidency for Bill Clinton. More
recently, Michael Steele served as
Chairman of the Republican Party during
2009-2011. Consequently, achieving the

aforementioned objectives should not be new territory. Rather, the creation and sustainment of a Black political party will mark the first time that we will fulfill these objectives strictly for ourselves as an important and significant player on America's political stage.

In a political world where million-dollar donors and political action committees rule the day, only large actions influence outcomes significantly.[42] A large action that Black Americans can implement to influence outcomes is to organize ourselves as a political party and to throw our political weight around as a sizeable voting bloc. Failure to adopt this approach may effectively limit considerably our voice in American

---

[42] See Confessore, Cohen, and Yourish (2015) and Higgins (2015).

politics despite possessing over 20
million eligible votes and serving as
the median voter.

Now is the time!

Too often in the marketplace of ideas
concerning Black Americans, those
participating in the dialogue pose
problems without proposing solutions.
In this case, the problem is that Black
Americans are not benefiting politically
as we should because we are not
leveraging our median voter status.
This essay proposes that we solve this
problem, at least in part, by establishing
a Black political party. The party would
enable us to organize ourselves and
establish a formal structure that should
permit us to bargain with the powers
that be — our votes in exchange for
political, economic, and social benefits
that we choose.

Of course, obtaining these potential results depends, in large measure, on the quality of our leadership. Organizing and sustaining a Black political party is no guarantee that these benefits will accrue. In other words, establishing a Black political party must be part of a broader indicator that we have achieved a certain degree of political maturity — including the ability to hold our leadership accountable.

It is our choice whether we take responsibility for making a Black political party a reality. Casual observation will tell us that other minority groups are leaning in this direction. If we and the broader nation stand by idly, we will find that not only have Hispanics formed their own political party, but that they will have also rewritten completely the political

demographic landscape in the form of
Latinofornia, New Latinico, Latinizonia,
Latinexas, and Latinorida.[43] We are
already close to the point where we look
up after two generations and find that
another immigrant group has entered
the US at the bottom of the socio-
economic ladder and has found its way
completely around us to a superior
political, economic, and social position.
If we are wise, then we will not allow
this to occur, but will form our own
political party, and then leverage it to
elevate our own position.

Time is moving on. The 2016 election
is around the corner. Let us not let it pass
without at least a serious discussion

---

[43] It was recently announced in the press
that Hispanics now exceed whites in the State of
California (see Panzar 2015).

about forming a Black political party.

Let us establish as a goal that 2020

should not come and go without the

realization and operationalization of

a Black political party.

The time for action is now!

References

Black, Duncan (1948). "On the Rationale
of Group Decision-making."
Journal of Political Economy. Vol.
56, No. 1; pp. 23-34.

Colby, Sandra and Jennifer Ortman
(2015). *Projections of the Size and
Composition of the US Population:
2014 to 2060*. Current Populations
Report PS25-1143. US Census
Bureau. Washington, DC.

Confessore, Nicholas, Sarah Cohen, and
Karen Yourish (2015). "Small Pool
of Rich Donors Dominate Election
Giving." *The New York Times*.
August 1. Accessed on August 5,
2015; http://www.nytimes.com/
2015/08/02/ us/small-pool-of-rich-

donors-dominates- election-giving.html?_r=0.

File, Thom (2015). Who Votes? Congressional Elections and The American Electorate: 1978-2014." *Population Characteristics*, P20-577. US Census Bureau. Washington, DC.

Higgins, Tim (2015). "Million-Dollar Donations Fuel Super-PAC's New Dominance." *Bloomberg*. July 31st. Accessed on August 5, 2015; http://www.bloomberg.com/politics/ articles/2015-08-01/million-dollar-donations- fuel-super-pacs-new-dominance.

Panzar, Javier (2015). "It's Official. Latinos Now Outnumber Whites in California." *Los Angeles Times*, July 8. Accessed on July 19, 2015; http://www.latimes.com/local/califor nia/la-me-census-latinos-20150708-story.html.

Pew Research Center (2012). *A Closer Look at the Parties in 2012*. Washington, DC. Accessed on August 5, 2016; http://www.people-

press.org/2012/08/23/a-closer-look-
at-the- parties-in-2012/.

Robinson, Eugene (2010).
*Disintegration: The Splintering of
Black America*. First Ancho Books.
New York.

Walton, Jr., Hanes (1972). *Black
Political Parties*." The Free Press.
New York.

_____ (1969). *The Negro in
Third Party Politics*. Dorrance &
Company. Philadelphia.

Brooks B. Robinson, Ph.D., completed
his undergraduate studies in economics
at the University of Wisconsin-Madison.
He completed Master's and Doctoral
Degrees in economics at George
Mason University, Fairfax, Virginia.
His most recent work is *Takeconomics:
A Counterintuitive Perspective* (2019).
He is author of two 2016 monographs:

The Case for Nation Formation and *21ˢᵗ Century Protests: A Handbook for Black America*. During 2009 and 2010, he published a trilogy: *Choice: Black America's Decision*, *Chosen: Black America's Calling*, and *Change: Black America's Religion*. Also, in 2009, he authored a ground-breaking article entitled, "Black Unemployment and Infotainment," in the January 2009 issue of the *Journal of Economic Inquiry*. He is founder, director, and chief developer of the website BlackEconomics.org, which addresses Black economic concepts, issues, policies, and plans.

Steal Away!

*A political analyst, writer and conserva-
tive commentator, Karl Miller calls for
"less resentment and more responsibility" from the black community.*

Less Resentment,
More Personal Responsibility

Karl Miller

A common narrative today by liberals
in politics and the media is that the
upward mobility of black Americans
has been constrained by the legacy of
slavery. However, America was not the
only country to have slavery. It is also
not the only country to have racism.
Every country has had elements of
racism even sometimes between color
tones of the same race. Many immigrants
of all colors have experienced hardships
in their former countries which no one
born in America, especially in the last 60

years, ever faced, but the immigrants
achieved great things once they lived
here. These include black immigrants
from war-torn parts of Africa that still
have elements of slavery, Eastern
Europeans from Albania or Kosovo
who experienced ethnic cleansing
and war, and immigrants from many
oppressive communist countries.

If slavery in America, which the
country fought a civil war to end over
150 year ago, was such a defining factor
of the prospects for black Americans
today, how come so many black
immigrants from other places such as
the Caribbean that also had slavery have
come America and done exceedingly
well? Millions of immigrants from all
over still seek to come to America. U.S
census data going back to the 1960s
show the earnings of black immigrants
from the Caribbean far outpacing those

of American blacks. In addition, among all groups, second-generation black West Indians have also been earning more than the U.S average.

Years ago, before I lived in America, I was fascinated why so many people from all over the world, including my native Jamaica and especially of color who grew up in poverty, could go to America and prosper. At the same time there was also a narrative about America being a "racist" country. I asked myself, "How could such a supposedly 'racist' country be so good for black immigrants?"

When I came to America and lived in the South Bronx, I observed many black Americans who had access to numerous welfare and affirmative action programs that was supposed to "help" them and contrasted that with many black immigrants who came to America

with virtually nothing but still
experienced rapid upward mobility.
More so, many of the poorest minority
majority communities were run by
Democrats for decades and even with
minority leaders.

What was also common was that the
Democrat Party, which had courted black
Americans as "the party for the "colored"
people, had also aggressively marketed
itself to new immigrants, especially of
color, with the same pitch. They
pandered to new arrivals with the idea,
"If you are an immigrant, you must
vote Democrat if you become a citizen
because everyone else is racist and do
not like you." Most black immigrants
still pursued achievement and
opportunities despite *prospective
barriers*, real or perceived.

However, from my observation,
the positive prospects of many black

Americans were destroyed by Democrats who pandered and used racial
scaremongering and victimhood to
constantly lock in their votes while not
delivering on the progress they promised
to deliver. The propensity by Democrats
to treat blacks perpetually as victims
also generationally suppressed the
ambition of many black Americans to
achieve despite the odds amongst them.
Many black families have been stuck in
welfare programs, bad schools, single
parent homes and high crime
neighborhoods for generations.

In addition, many Democrats,
while pandering to black and poor
neighborhoods, often do garner the votes
but give preferences to special interests
like teachers' unions at the expense of
opportunities for black and poor
neighborhoods. For example, in South
Bronx and other poor neighborhoods,

charter schools have proven to offer
a better quality and more upwardly
mobility educational path for black
and other minority children. However,
Democrats have consistently choked
off or capped the number of charter
schools to satisfy teachers unions
who are a huge donor base for those
Democrats. Tens of thousands of
minority families desperately call for
lifting the cap on charters to better serve
their children. The NY Post reported last
April that 17,234 kids in the South Bronx
had to compete for only 4,453 seats in
charter schools. While Democrats often
purport to be civil right and social justice
warriors for blacks, they play a major
role in restricting the opportunities for
blacks with their constant opposition to
better quality education for them by
opposing charters.

The policies of the Democrat progressive left have failed blacks and many constituencies for so long and often that the most expeditious political path to maintain their votes is constant racial fear mongering. Democrats have now combined that with attacks on law enforcement, lobbying for reparations for blacks and challenging the founding ideas of America as racist. Black Americans are being served even worst by black politicians who stoke racial grievance as an identity politics crutch to boost their own political careers. 2020 presidential contender Kamala Harris who has tried to tout her law career took to Twitter to falsely allege that the Michael Brown was "murdered" by police in Ferguson, Missouri, even though the Obama justice investigation (under the direction of the black Attorney General, Eric Holder) clearly showed

that Brown had posed a threat to Officer
Wilson after attacking him in his police
car.

An often-overlooked line in the
speech which the Rev. Martin Luther
King Jr. delivered in front of the Lincoln
Memorial at the 1963 March on
Washington reads: "When the architects
of our Great Republic wrote the
magnificent words of the Constitution
and the Declaration of Independence,
they were signing a promissory note to
which every American was to fall heir."
And in his famous Gettysburg Address,
Abraham Lincoln spoke of America as
"dedicated to the proposition that all men
are created equal."

The founding principles and ideas
of liberty and prosperity were not only
genius and still relevant, but also a
constant topic of discussion by
America's founders in the *Federalist*

Papers in the conversation on determining the limits on the powers of those who seek it in government. They noted, "Man is not infallible and thus subject to fault." When the left today try to mischaracterize the founding ideas as racist and outdated, they should be reminded that the truths of the founding ideas of prosperity and liberty for all still hold, but they are also constrained by the ever-present truth cautioned by the founders about the self-ambitious motives of the "not infallible" who seek power.

The narrative of racial resentment being advocated by the left, the media and Democrat politicians is not only dangerous and undermining to the vast improvements in racial equality and race relations achieved in the last decades; it also discourages the ambition to succeed in those they purport to help. The black

community has to take more
responsibility to not constantly give their
votes to people who constantly take it for
granted.

Karl Miller is a political analyst,
writer and conservative commentator.
His writings, which cover a wide range
of domestic and foreign policy topics and
political events, are published on shis
website: karlmiller.org

An immigrant from Jamaica, Karl's
journey in conservatism began at a young
age long before he became an American
citizen. He was inspired by America's
founding ideas that made the American
Dream for millions a reality, and the
importance of America's role in the
world to defend freedom. His writings
often ask why conservative ideas such
as limited government, strong national

security and economic freedom are
relevant to defend and promote liberty
and opportunity in the 21st century.

He has been a political opinion
writer at examiner.com and has
contributed pieces to
westernjournalism.com and also E21,
the economics portal of The Manhattan
Institute for Policy Research. He has
also appeared on the FOX News Hannity
show special on black conservatives.

He is also the author of an upcoming
eBook, *Thoughts and Proposals
from a Conservative Immigrant –
The Framework of Bills to Reform
Immigration and Why Conservative
Immigrants Will be Crucial to Prevent
Socialism in America.*

*An IT Specialist in Higher education
with over 20 years of experience in IT,
Vice President for the Maryland
Federation of Republican Women
(MFRW) and President of the Repub-
lican Club of Frederick County,
and a recipient of the Maryland
Republican Woman of the Year, Marie
Fischer explains how the Democrat
Party has prevented black children
from getting a quality education.*

School Choice Should be
a *Right* and Not a *Want*

Marie Fischer

If you ask any middle-class Black
American what the one thing was your
parents emphasized when you were
growing, almost all of us would say,
"getting a good education." Most of us
constantly heard how important it was to

get a good education. Many Black parents then and now would sacrifice anything and everything for that education. Due to various circumstances, many of these same parents may not have had an education themselves, but they would move "hell and highwater" so their children would. That being said, I still cannot fathom how many Black Americans, especially parents of school age children, will still vote Democrat since this party has done so much to prevent Black children from getting a quality education, especially in the public school system, via school choice.

Let me rephrase that: the National Education Association (NEA) and the American Federation of Teachers (AFT) are two of the biggest advocates against school choice vouchers, tax credits scholarships, Education Savings accounts, and charter schools. They push this agenda by funding Democrat candidates who will vote the way they want. Both the NEA and the AFT two of the top 30 donors to Democrat candidates with each donating approximately 89% and 100%, respectively, of their campaign funding to Democrat candidates and Liberal causes. Both the NEA and AFT, through the Democrat officials they fund and support, push a narrative that the US public school system is the best for all students by disavowing not only the voucher system, but even charter schools, whose concept was created by public school teachers in the first place. They state that the various choices take money away from the public school system. In reality, what they really mean is there will be less money going towards their coffers in the end. If a teacher could get a better salary and/or better working conditions at a private or charter school then they may choose to work there. This means the teachers will no longer need to be a part of a dues paying teachers union, which means less funds for the union coffers.

Our current state of public education, especially for many Black students, is probably worse than it was before *Brown vs Board of Education*. Parents then were fighting to be able to send their children to schools in their neighborhood instead of the segregated schools across town. Now these neighborhood schools are worse than the segregated schools' children used to attend! The many years of Democrat policies have trapped these families, especially children, in failing school districts. There are no options of even choice within the public school system, let alone a voucher system to allow the students the option of going to a private school.

Time and time again, we read stories about how Black and Hispanic children in various charter schools around the country are not only meeting the achievement standards but surpassing them. There are schools such as Urban Prep in Chicago, which has had 100% of their seniors admitted to college for over seven years in a row. Schools like Success Academy in Crown Heights in Brooklyn, where 100% of the students (90% Black and Hispanic) scored at the proficient level in Math (in NYS only 39% of all student score at proficient). In Florida, Black charter school students are scoring 4% better than their peers in standard public schools on standardized reading tests.

There are many who wonder why I fight so hard for school choice. (School choice was the main plank of my platform when I ran for the Frederick County Board of Education in the Spring of 2018.) I fight hard for school choice because I am a product of school choice. I know I would not be where I am today if my parents did not get that option in the mid-70's.

I grew up in a lower-middle class family of four. Our neighborhood was one that changed from being majority white in the 60's to majority Black by the mid-80's and was populated by older retired residents who were part of the Black middle class (mostly retired teachers, postal workers plus a retired Negro league star, Joe B. Scott). Unfortunately, the neighborhood elementary school I was initially assigned to was not what my parents wanted in terms of a good education.

During this time my father was attempting to complete his education at Memphis State University (now University of Memphis) when he came across an elementary school on the college campus. The school he stumbled upon (and which would eventually be my and my sister's elementary school) was called MSU Campus school. Admission to the school was tiered. Students of faculty and staff as well as siblings of current students had first choice, students of the college had second choice, neighborhood children had third choice, and whatever spots were left were up for grabs by anyone within the city limits.

At Campus school students are individually guided, and you reach *your*

potential, not the classroom's potential.
Because students went at their own pace
and were challenged not only by teachers
but by each other, I left the school
performing seventh grade English and
eighth grade Math.

Almost everyone one who went
through Campus school was admitted
into the Optional program for the
Memphis City Schools System. The
Optional program is the closest example
of a pure choice model in a public
school system. Although it has changed
greatly from when I attended the schools
in Memphis, once you were in the
Optional program, you could choose
(if there was space) to transfer between
schools that were in the program.

Although I attended a great middle
school and high school, I was allowed to
switch to a different school for the last

two years of high school. My new school offered a class in etymology which not only improved my vocabulary but improved both my PSAT and SAT test scores. The increase in scores allowed me to be a National Achievement Finalist, which led to me getting additional scholarships when I applied to various college and when I attended NYU. None of this would have be possible without my parents and me having a choice in my education. I believe educational choice in K-12 allows children and parents to have more available choices throughout their life.

I have always wondered how quick Democrat leaders and officials (as well as their NEA and AFT supporters) would change their minds about school choice if there was none for their children. If their offspring were forced to attend schools that many Black children attend today, how would they react? Would there still be schools that lack educational resources as well as basic resources (some schools in Baltimore City lack not only air conditioning for the late spring and early fall, but many also lack heat in the winter.) or would a choice system be set up for all children to access a true quality education. If that were done, a student's lack of success would solely be on their shoulders and not blamed upon their circumstances.

I leave you with one final reason I support school choice. I have a 17-year-old son who is a senior in high school who is taking a number of college courses his senior year of high school. If I had not made the decision to use all of my child support each month when he was younger (with the approval of his dad) to place him in a Yeshiva (a private religious Jewish school), he would not be at this point in his education. You see my son was diagnosed as being on the Autism spectrum at the age of five because the school he attended did not write him off as another Black child who was just difficult and had behavior issues. He was seen as a bright and intelligent boy whose behavior was a manifestation of a learning problem. In fact, when he was initially tested in the public school system (they did a large number of the education testing in the town) he tested off the chart academically. My son's school pushed back and asked for more testing. It was then he was diagnosed as being on the spectrum. In the town we lived in, children with any form of learning issues were sent to one special education school

that was not in the best neighborhood.
This school housed children with
legitimate learning issue as well as those
who deal with mental issues, a recipe
for educational disaster for all. I made
an educational choice for my son and it
affected me financially then. G-d willing,
it will benefit not only myself and my
son, but all of society because now he is
an educated young Black man with
unlimited potential.

Sources

Camera, L. (2017, July 5). Teachers
Union Adopts New, Anti-Charter
School Policy. Retrieved from
https://www.usnews.com/news/educ
ation-news/articles/2017-07-
05/teachers-union-adopts-new-anti-
charter-school-policy.

Center for Responsive Politics. (2019,
September 21). Teachers Unions.
Retrieved from

https://www.opensecrets.org/industri
es/indus.php?cycle=2020&ind=L13
00.

EdChoice. (2019, January 18).
Arguments For and Against School
Choice in 2017. Retrieved from
https://www.edchoice.org/blog/argu
ments-for-and-against-school-
choice-2017/.

Fair, T. W. (2017, September 21).
School choice is crucial for African-
American students' success.
Retrieved from
https://www.usatoday.com/story/opi
nion/2017/09/21/school-choice-
crucial-african-american-students-
success-t-willard-fair-
column/665451001/.

Finley, T. (2016, April 28). 100 Percent
of Seniors at Chicago School
Admitted to College For 7th Year
in A Row. Retrieved from
https://www.huffpost.com/entry/100
-percent-of-seniors-at-chicago-
school-admitted-to-college-for-7th-
year-in-a-
row_n_5722273ee4b0b49df6aa5aaa.

Sharma, R. (2016, September 1). Top Democrat Donors. Retrieved September 29, 2019, from https://www.investopedia.com/news /top-democrat-donors/.

Sowell, T. (2016, August 18). Does Black Success Matter? Retrieved from https://www.nationalreview. com/2016/08/charter-schools-benefit-blacks-and-help-all-minorities-succeed/.

The Case Against Vouchers. (n.d.). Retrieved from http://www.nea.org /home/19133.htm.

Marie Fischer, originally from Memphis, Tennessee, is a resident of Frederick County, Maryland, where she was a 2018 primary candidate for the Frederick County Board of Education. Marie is an IT Specialist in higher education with over 20 years of experience in IT and has worked as a freelance political consultant on various

State of Maryland campaigns. She
attended NYU, has a degree in Liberal
Arts, and is currently pursuing
a second degree in Communications.
Ms. Fischer is currently serving as the
third Vice President for the Maryland
Federation of Republican Women
(MFRW) and is the President of the
Republican Club of Frederick County.
She is also a member of Project 21,
an initiative of The National Center
for Public Policy Research to promote
the views of Black Americans whose
entrepreneurial spirit, dedication to
family and commitment to individual
responsibility have not traditionally
been echoed by the nation's civil rights
establishment. This past May, Marie
received the Diana Waters Maryland
Republican Woman of the Year for 2018
by the Maryland State Republican Party.

*The last contribution is from John
Jocelyn, a prominent conservative
thinker, teacher, minister, and life coach
who asks that blacks open their minds
and listen to people with new ideas.*

Blacks Need to be Open to New Ideas

John M. Jocelyn

Don Lemon of the Cable News
Network (CNN) and many other liberal
generals have challenged the notion
of freedom of thought within the black
community. In broad daylight, I watched
the leadership at CNN give complete
license to silence the voice of an African
American icon, Kanye West, i.e.,
"a high-tech lynching" (in the words
of Supreme Court Justice Clarence
Thomas). The network gives complete
freedom to liberals of all stripes to
disparage conservatives and use vile

language against them. "We can respect his opinion, but we don't have to respect his ignorance," Lemon said (Schwartz, 2018).

The African American actor Samuel L. Jackson and Don Lemon figuratively called for a gauntlet to line up and prevent West's ability to express himself in support of conservatism. In reference to West, Lemon said, "It's like a word salad where you realize that Kanye West, entitled to his own opinion, but is not very bright and not very — he — when — I'm talking about this issue, not overall, but when it comes to these issues, he's not clued in" (Schwartz, 2018).

Anyone listening to West realizes that he has two central themes: the importance of appreciating diverse ideas and the need for respect for various paths toward progress. These notions are like a passing wind in the understanding of the liberal king makers. Still, West has stated his political philosophy over and over.

Let's assume that we lived in a world dominated by Don Lemon of CNN, and that he is the sole voice of black people. We are asked to listen to him on a daily basis to ensure our indoctrination. Lemon makes his presentation in an attempt to ensure that we understand our place and that we should allow him and other members of the "brilliant liberal elites" to do all the thinking. According to Lemon, all black people must disagree with Kanye West. The fact is that there was never a time, until recently, when black ideas were monolithic on one strand.

Why is it so important to control the mindset of the black community? In reality, the agenda is not so much with Mr. West but rather the larger

African American public. Most people, nevertheless, agree that having various views is essential for the growth of a community. The growth of any community requires open discussion and appreciation of any challenges to the status quo.

The #walkaway movement[44] is punching a hole directly in the center of this censoring of conservative ideas among black Americans. The whole idea of the #walkaway movement is the willingness to challenge liberal orthodoxy and examine political views for their effectiveness. A young African American named C.J. Pearson wrote, "The Democratic Party is the party of slavery. The party of Jim Crow. The party of segregation. The party of the

---

[44] The WalkAway campaign is a social media campaign whose stated goal was to "encourage others to walk away from the "divisive" left, but also to take back the narrative from the "liberal" media about what it means to be a conservative in America." [Source: Wikipwdia.com]

KKK. Democrats walked away from
black folks long ago. Now, it's our time
to #Walkaway" (Pearson, 2018). This
young man realizes a profound notion,
stagnation requires reflection and a
deeper challenge to the normal expected
view of the world. Grow requires that
we challenge everything and anything
which stands in the way of progress

The black conservative understands
that the free-flow of ideas is crucial for
the development of a vibrant and
healthy community. It does not take
a brain scientist to know that freedom
of expression is essential for any
community. We survive by following
normalcy, but we strive breakdown every
factor which we deemed normal and
demanded. The rules must be challenged
and demanded an openness for new and
vibrant manner of thinking. The key in
preventing our usage in a political game
lies in the free flowing of idea and a
constant challenge of the status from any

political party in relation to our standing. We must never allow ourselves to become a tool in pushing someone else's agenda.

Sources

Pearson, C.J. (2018). *Twitter*. Retrieved from https://twitter.com/thecjpearson

Schwartz, I. (2018, August 30). Don Lemon: Kanye West "Not Very Bright". *RealClear Politics*. Retrieved from https://www.realclearpolitics. com/video/2018/08/30/ don_lemon_kanye_west_ not_very_bright.html

John Jocelyn is a prominent
conservative thinker, teacher, minister,
and life coach who is dedicated to
making a difference in the lives of others.
Between his military service in the U.S.
Air Force and his work with many non-
profits that work to help families and
children see the best of life, Jocelyn's
humanitarian and philanthropic efforts
are well known in his community.

He seeks to take these works one step
further, as an offering to the general
public, by contributing to this much-
needed book on conservative philosophy.

About the Editor

Richard Showstack is a freelance writer, author, and editor in Southern California. He decided to undertake this project because he wanted to draw attention to all of the harm Democratic Party policies have done to the black community over the past 50 years and to suggest an alternative.

His other books include

➤ *A HORSE NAMED PEGGY and Other Enchanting character-building Stories for Smart Teenage Boys Who Want to Grow Up to Be Good Men,*

➤ *THE GIFT OF MAGIC and Other Enchanting character-building Stories for Smart Teenage Girls Who Want to Grow Up to Be Strong Women*

➤ *ePIFfunnies: Humorous Reflections, Insights, and Musings on Life and Living,*

➢ *Son of ePIFfunnies: More Humorous Reflections, Insights, and Musings on Life and Living.*

➢ *The Crossword Puzzlers Handbook: Over 1,500 Words You Need to Know*

➢ *How Evolution Works….and why it matters to us*

To contact Richard, email him at:

ToStealAway@AOL.com

Notes:

1) The same as for all those who contributed essays to this book, Richard Showstack is not being paid for his work.

2) Any profits from this book will be donated to Candace Owens' "Blexit Foundation" and James Golden's "New Journey" PAC.